SARASOTA

Chef du Jour

SARASOTA

Chef du Jour

COOK BOOK
OF CHEF RECIPES

15th Anniversary Edition

By Jan McCann
and featuring Judi Gallagher

Strawberry Press, Sarasota, Florida

Cover Art:
Joné Ritchie

Cover Design:
Joanie Phieffer

Photography:
Linda Thomas

1st Printing 1992, 1000 copies
2nd Printing 1993, 2000 copies
3rd Printing 1994, 3000 copies
4th Printing 1995, 3000 copies
5th Printing 1997, 3000 copies
6th Printing 1999, 3000 copies
7th Printing 2003, 3000 copies
8th Printing 2007, 3500 copies

ISBN 0-9764995-0-9
Copyright 1992

Strawberry Press, 3712 Woodmont Drive, Sarasota, FL 34232 941-377-9786

To all my friends and family,
especially the love of my life,
Kim McCann

Acknowledgements

This being my 8th edition, one would think that a routine would develop over 4 or 5 or 6 editions, but for me such is not the case. This one was much more a collaborative effort. I had all my close friends involved in this edition. My "regular job", puts me on the road away from Sarasota most of the week. This is why you will notice recipes from as far south as Naples. My friends Linda Thomas and Judi Gallagher assisted in acquiring recipes. My mom helped proof read. Without their assistance this edition would not have been possible.

Susan Caamano also took part in typing recipes and proofreading. Linda Thomas and Susan also helped testing recipes. I am really confident you will get rave reviews with these recipes that the Chef's of Southwest Florida have put forth.

It has been a pleasure working with my friend and co-host Judi Gallagher. I think you will find the addition of Judi's influence and recipes makes this 15th anniversary edition the most special of all.

Special thanks to Marjorie North, Marsha Fottler and Françoise O'Neil for contributing their favorite recipes to me. These girls are well known writers in Southwest Florida and I think they add a wonderful variety to this edition.

Last but not least, thank you to all the Chefs that contributed recipes to make this book possible.

Contents

Foreward

By Judi Gallagher

Approximately 15 years ago my husband and I ventured from snowy Boston to the warmth of Sarasota, Florida for a brief respite from the harsh New England winter. While wandering St Armand's Circle, we came upon a gift store selling the **Chef Du Jour** Cookbook: its inaugural edition. Being a professional chef, I loved the recipes with a hint of Florida sunshine on almost every page and the flavors of local chefs accenting the selections like a fine seasoning. Little did I know that many years later, after relocating to Sarasota permanently, Jan McCann and I would become good friends.

For me, The **Chef Du Jour** Cookbook has become an annual gift for friends both locally and throughout the country. Jan's professional respect from the chefs is always apparent and the cookbook invites anyone from any level of cooking skill to relax and enjoy these wonderful selections. For sure, the book's ease, intimacy and caliber mirror the high standards of the author.

I am truly honored to be a part of this special anniversary edition. When Jan and I first designed the "In the Kitchen with Judi and Jan" we discovered our love of old family recipes and their anectodotal kitchen guidance. Over many a steaming pot of Vietnamese Noodle Bowls we reminisced about our grandmothers' secret ingredients and the recipes that we have both gathered from such great professionals as Jacques Pe'pin and Roy Yamaguchi. We realized this collaborative chapter simultaneously represented our friendship and love of food. Throughout the past years, several recipes from this creative collection have been re-created for my cooking shows, always enhancing the program with technique and flawless flavors.

Jan's passion for food and artistry of presenting our local chefs' recipes are a keepsake for us all!

Introductions

WELCOME!! Come on in, sit down and read a few chapters. If you are already familiar with **Chef Du Jour** then you are in for a treat because this is my 8th edition and I am celebrating 15 years of publishing. My first edition was printed back in 1992. First printing was 1000. Now I'm printing 3500.

Meet my celebrity friend Judi Gallagher. Judi is the hostess of Cooking in Paradise, which airs Saturday and Sunday on channel 6 SNN and weekdays on channel 20 from 7:30 to 8 o'clock p.m. Judi also hosts a radio show by the same name on 1620 AM and writes for Sarasota Magazine. Judi is a very busy lady to say the least. Judi is a big supporter of charities and is a fabulous hostess for many fund raising events. If you would like to get to know more about Judi go to her web site cookinginparadise.com

I hope you start to notice the difference and variety of palm trees in our tropical locale. This is the result of the influence from my friend Linda Thomas. She shared her knowledge. Now I have a mutual appreciation and love of palms as well. Linda is a great friend and photographer. She shot all the photos of palms in this edition.

All new, all fresh, and I think with more of a tropical flavor. Everywhere I go when I mention I am from Sarasota the reply is that they love Sarasota. There is just something about this area that makes you want to stay. If you are visiting take the flavors home with you. If you are lucky enough to live here you know these Chefs. Invite friends over and bite into the excellent cuisine of Sarasota **Chef Du Jour.**

Appetizers & Brunch

Photo Linda Thomas

Bottle Palm

Orchid sculpture at the entrance of Selby Gardens

Pecan Crusted Bacon

Heide Jaeger-Drum

Serves 12 – 14

Always a big hit, never one piece left over. Regular smoked bacon works best. Pre-cooked bacon does not work.

Combine for topping:

1/4 cup brown sugar, packed
1 tsp. flour
1/2 cup pecans or walnuts, coarsely chopped.

Heide will sometimes double the amount of the topping.

🖋 Place 1 pound of bacon strips separated and halved on a foil lined rimmed cooking sheet. The bacon should touch but not overlap.

🖋 Sprinkle with the topping and bake at 350° for about 30 minutes, until the bacon looks nice and crisp. Drain on paper towels and serve warm.

The Sandbar

100 Spring Ave
Anna Maria, FL 34216
941-778-0444

Spinach and Artichoke Dip

Chef Ian Fairweather

Serves 4

1 lb. spinach
2 cups artichoke hearts
1 cup chopped onions
1 tsp. olive oil
1 lb. cream cheese
1 cup milk
1 cup heavy cream
2 cups shredded pepper jack cheese
1 tsp. granulated garlic
1 tsp. cayenne pepper
1 bread bowl.

Garnish:

1 cup cheddar cheese
2 oz. chopped tomato
1 oz. green onion

Heat olive oil in a pan. Sauté onion until tender. Add milk

and cream. Bring to a simmer. Add cream cheese and pepper jack cheese. Melt down and add spinach and artichokes.

Season with garlic and cayenne pepper to taste. Hollow out round loaf of bread and reserve bread. Ladle spinach mixture into bread bowl. Sprinkle with cheddar cheese on top and place in 350° oven until cheddar melts.

Place on plate and garnish with tomato and green onion. Serve with extra pieces of bread arranged around the dish for dipping.

Entrance to Bay Front Park

Greer's Grill

6566 Gateway Ave.
Sarasota, FL 34231
In Gulf Gate Village
941-926-0606

Brie and Artichoke Dip

Chef Jeff Yoakum

Serves 6

> 1 can artichoke hearts
> 2 wheels of Brie
> 1/4 cup white wine

- Sauté artichokes with white wine and 1 wheel of Brie until the cheese is melted.

- Pour into casserole dish and top with slices of Brie from the second wheel.

- Bake in 450° oven for 5 minutes or until golden brown. Serve with toasted pita bread

Galileo

1538 Stickney Point Road
In the Boatyard Village
Sarasota, FL 34231
941-927-9600

Galileo Lobster Dip

Chef Thomas M. Harvey

Serves 4

8 oz. cooked and chopped cold water lobster meat
8 oz. Mascarpone cheese
1 oz minced onion

Topping:

1 cup Japanese breadcrumbs
3 tbsp. softened butter
1 tsp. minced garlic
1 tbsp chopped parsley
salt and pepper

Mix all topping ingredients together making sure breadcrumbs are well coated with butter.

Mix lobster, onion and mascarpone and place in a shallow baking dish, perhaps a crème brulee dish.

Top with breadcrumb mixture and bake in 350° oven for 30 to 40 minutes until topping is golden and mixture is hot. Do not over bake, as cheese will separate with excessive heat. Serve with crostini, (toasted bread points).

Fleming's Steakhouse and Wine Bar

2001 Siesta Drive
Sarasota, FL 34239
941-358-9463

Salmon Bruschetta

Chef Russell Skall

Serves 4

8 slices French baguette
8 tbsp. cream cheese spread
4 oz. smoked salmon
4 whole garlic cloves
1 oz. olive oil
3 oz. sun dried tomatoes
1 tbsp. red onion
5 fresh basil leaves
pinch of Kosher salt and finely ground black pepper

Cut baguette into bias cuts ½ inch thick and 4" long. Place in 350° oven for 5 minutes to toast.

Soften cream cheese and spread on toasted bread. Spread smoked salmon over cream cheese.

8

- Cook garlic in olive oil in sauté pan on medium high heat for 4 –5 minutes till lightly brown. Pull from heat and immediately drain oil and reserve.

- Rough-cut tomatoes into ¼" pieces.

- Rough-cut cooked garlic and add to the tomatoes.

- Mince onion, cut basil leaves into thin ribbons and add to bowl.

- Combine cooking oil, kosher salt and black pepper, mix to incorporate.

- Spoon sun dried tomato relish over the salmon and serve.

Fountain at Pineapple and Lemon

Bellagio Ristorante

322 S. Washington Blvd.
Sarasota, FL 34237
941-330-1300

Mama Giuliva's Bruschetta

Chef Joe Dante

Serves 6 - 8

3 firm ripe tomatoes – chopped small dice
2 slices red onion – very small dice
8 – 10 mint leaves – chopped
1/2 cup olive oil
2 tbsp. balsamic vinegar
1 French baguette (loaf of bread)

🍃 Mix tomatoes, red onions, mint, olive oil and balsamic vinegar together.

🍃 Slice French baguette diagonally ½ inch thick. Brush with olive oil. Sprinkle with salt and pepper. Toast lightly in 350° oven.

🍃 Let cool and top with tomato mixture.

Island Gourmet

201 Venice Avenue
Venice, FL 34285
941-485-1668

Corn & Crab Salad on Pita or Endive Leaf

Heide Jaeger-Drum

Serves 30 - 35

A cool refreshing summertime appetizer, and if served on some lettuce greens, also a great salad. Two of the ingredients, the corn and the crab, are just naturals for pairing with chardonnay.

Cream together:
¼ cup cream cheese, or cheese mixed with sour cream
¼ cup scallions, thinly sliced
½ jalapeno, seeded and chopped fine
2 tbsp. lemon juice
1 tsp. cumin
1 tsp. salt and pepper to taste
some cayenne pepper or "Old Bay" seasoning

Blend in:
6 oz. crabmeat
½ cup fresh corn kernels

Re-season and chill up to one day ahead of time.

Serve with toasted pita chips or in an endive leaf.

To make pita chips: Cut pita bread into wedges and seperate the two sides. Brush with olive oil and sprinkle salt to add some flavor. If cooled completely before bagging, they last for days.

Marie's Italian Kitchen

5767 Beneva Road
Sarasota, FL 34233
941-923-1000

Caponata alla Siciliana (Sweet & Sour Eggplant)

Bill Wells

Serves 12

- Peel and cut **2 eggplants** into ½ inch cubes.

- Place them in a colander, salt generously and let stand for one hour.

- Wash, dry and fry in a small amount of **olive oil** over moderate heat, stirring from time to time until they are lightly browned. Remove and set aside. Fry in olive oil until soft **2 cups of chopped celery** and **1 cup chopped onion**. Return the eggplant and add **2 cups of chopped plum tomatoes**.

- Simmer and stir from time to time for 20 minutes.

- Put eggplant mixture in a bowl. To that add **3 tablespoons of capers, 2 tablespoons of pine nuts,** a dozen chopped or broken **green olives** and a dozen chopped or broken **black olives**.

- Mix **1/2 cup red wine vinegar** with **4 teaspoons of sugar** and add to eggplant mixture. **Salt and pepper** to taste and stir, cover and place in refrigerator.

Let stand an hour or so then taste. Add more vinegar or sugar as needed. Return to refrigerator and let stand overnight to let the flavors marry.

This should be served at room temperature as an appetizer or sandwich filling.

This recipe best made a day or two ahead. Delicious!!

Sculpture at Five Points, Downtown Sarasota

The Beach House

200 Gulf Drive North
Bradenton Beach, FL 34218
941-779-2222

Stuffed Portabella Mushrooms

Makes 4 large mushrooms

Hand pick 4 large portabella mushrooms, the size of a coffee saucer

- Remove the stem and carefully scrape the gills from the under side of the cap and discard
- Cook the mushroom caps by steaming, poaching or even grilling for added flavor. It is your choice. Cook the caps until the flesh is slightly tender. Some caps are thick and need to be partially cooked. Allow to cool.
- Have on hand 4 slices of ordinary white bread.

The stuffing:

     1 lb. shrimp, cooked
     8 oz. pepper jack cheese
     ½ cup mayonnaise
     1 whole egg
     ¼ cup tomato, diced
     1 tbsp. scallions, finely chopped
     1 cup Japanese bread crumbs, (Panko)
     1 tsp. salt and pepper
     1 tsp. granulated garlic
     dash of Tabasco sauce

- Blend all ingredients with cooked shrimp. Stuffing should be very moist but tacky and should hold a molded form.

14

- Divide the stuffing into 4 equal parts. Flip the mushroom caps stem side up.
- Fill the mushroom caps with the stuffing. Cut white bread into small cubes. Arrange the bread cubes on top of the moist stuffing.
- Brush bread cubes with butter and season with paprika.
- Bake the mushrooms uncovered in 450 - 500° oven for 8 - 10 minutes or until topping is golden.

The crisp topping offers a nice contrast in texture to the rich stuffing and tender mushroom.

At the corner of Coconut and Gulf Stream Ave.

15

Sean Beauchamp Brady

Italian Cookbook Author, Italian Culinary tour guide & Sarasota Resident

Polpette di Pollo "alla Romana"
(Chicken Meatballs wrapped in Prosciutto and Sage)

I called these chicken meatballs "alla Romana" because they remind me of the classic Saltimbocca alla Romana. This traditional main course, found on almost all Roman menus, is a veal cutlet topped with Prosciutto and sage sautéed quickly in butter. ("Saltimbocca" means jump in the mouth.) The chicken in this cocktail version remains amazingly moist because of the milk soaked bread. The ham not only crisps up to form a heavenly crust, but also lends its intense flavor to the meatball within.

½ cup milk
4 slices sturdy white bread , crusts removed
     (Pepperidge Farm is recommended)
1 ½ lbs. ground chicken (or turkey) mixed light and dark meat
2 tbsp. grated Parmigiano-Reggiano, Pecorino-Romano, or
     Grana Padano cheese
1 egg, beaten
1 tsp. salt, or to taste
¼ tsp. black pepper, or to taste
A few gratings of nutmeg
18-20 fresh sage leaves
⅓ lb. Prosciutto, sliced thin
1 tbsp. butter

🌿 In a shallow bowl, soak the bread in milk until soft, about 5 minutes. Remove the bread and squeeze out any excess milk. In a large mixing bowl, combine the bread, chicken, cheese, egg, salt, pepper, and nutmeg. Mix with your hands until the mixture is well combined.

🌿 Place several pieces of Prosciutto onto a cutting board. Slice each piece into 3 or 4 smaller pieces about 3 by 2 inches. Place a sage leaf in the center of each of these new smaller pieces.

🌿 Place a bowl of cold water near your work surface for dipping your hands. With wet hands, take about 2 tbsp. of the meat mixture and form oval patties. Place a patty over the sage leaf in the center of each Prosciutto piece. Carefully wrap the sides of the Prosciutto up around each patty. The Prosciutto does not have to completely surround the chicken.

🌿 In a large skillet, heat the butter over medium heat. Fry the meatballs, seam side down for five minutes, until the Prosciutto is crisp and is beginning to brown. Using two spoons, carefully flip the patties and cook the underside for 4-5 minutes until the meatballs are fully cooked. Serve warm or at room temperature.

Note: The meatballs can be prepared ahead, and kept covered in the refrigerator for two days before cooking. If you cook them ahead, reheat for about a minute on each side in a skillet set over medium heat. Reheating in a microwave is not recommended.

Wine suggestions:
Serve these with a crisp glass of Frascati from the hills outside Rome.

Cru

1377 Main Street
Sarasota, FL 34236
941-951-NAPA

Cru's Crab Cakes

Chef Malin Parker

> 1 lb. blue crab meat
> 1/4 cup yellow onion, small dice
> 2 tsp. garlic, minced
> 1/2 tbsp. Old Bay seasoning
> 1/2 tbsp. Dijon mustard
> 1/2 cup mayonnaise
> 1/2 cup Japanese breadcrumbs

🍃 Combine ingredients in a mixing bowl. Mix delicately being careful not to break up the crab, but to combine the ingredients.

🍃 Form into cakes, 4 oz in weight.

🍃 Dredge in additional Japanese breadcrumbs.

🍃 Fry in 350° oil until golden brown.

This recipe is special to me because it is the "one" that I am asked for most frequently. I am almost embarrassed to give it out because I am a Chef and it should be this really complicated "thing" but the truth is it is extremely simple. However, the simplicity of it really highlights the crab (imagine that!). If you have the opportunity, try using blue crab from the St. John's River from Jacksonville, Florida.

The Turtle Club *of Historic Punta Gorda*

139 W. Marion Ave.
Punta Gorda, FL 33950
941-637-9477

Turtle Crab Cakes

Tony Gonzalez

> 1 lb. lump crabmeat
> 1/2 cup bread crumbs
> 1 ½ tbsp. chopped parsley
> 1 tbsp. Old Bay seasoning
> 2/3 cup mayonnaise
> 1/3 cup Dijon mustard
> juice from ½ Lemon

🍃 Mix crabmeat, Japanese breadcrumbs & parsley together. Be careful not to completely break crab apart.

🍃 Add Dijon mustard, mayonnaise & Old Bay seasoning. Toss gently until just mixed. Add lemon juice & let rest 15 minutes.

🍃 Form cakes (8 or 9 2 oz. cakes)

🍃 Heat skillet over medium flame. Add olive oil & sear crabcakes for about 1 ½ minutes on each side. Finish in 300° oven for 5 - 8 minutes.

🍃 Serve over mixed greens with your favorite vinaigrette or as part of a fresh seafood platter.

19

Mediterraneo

1970 Main Street
Sarasota, FL 34236
941-365-4122

Tuna Carpaccio

Gianluca DiCostanzo

Serves 6 - 10

> 4 lbs. sushi grade tuna
> 4 lbs. salt
> 3 lbs. sugar
> 4 grapefruit
> 5 lemons
> 6 oranges
> 6 stalks fennel
> 1 gallon milk
> 1 liter extra virgin olive oil

🍃 Mix salt and sugar in a large pan. Put tuna in pan and coat with salt and sugar mixture. Peel oranges and lemons and put rinds on top of tuna (save lemon pulp after peeling). Refrigerate tuna for 24 hours.

🍃 After 24 hours, wash tuna with water and dry well. In another pan, place tuna and cover completely with milk. Refrigerate again for 12 hours.

✎ After 12 hours, rinse and dry tuna. Heat oil in skillet on medium-high heat and quickly sear tuna on both sides. Allow tuna to cool.

✎ To serve, slice tuna very thin and place on outer edges of a flat plate. In the center of plate, place thinly sliced fennel topped with peeled grapefruit slices. Squeeze lemon juice and mix with a small amount of olive oil and drizzle on top of carpaccio and fennel.

Serve with a dry white wine.

Mediterraneo Building

Javier's Steakhouse and Wine Bar

6621 Midnight Pass Road
Sarasota, FL 34242
941-349-1792

Ceviche de Corvina

Peru's most famous appetizer! Fresh Pacific coast Corvina marinated with lime juice, red onions, sweet red and green peppers and a touch of Peruvian aji pepper.

Serves 6 - 10

> 3 to 4 pounds corvina, cubed or other mild white fish
> juice of 10 lemons
> juice of 2 limes
> 1/2 bunch celery, thinly sliced
> 1 large red pepper, julienne
> 1 large green pepper, julienne
> 1 large red onion, diced
> 1 tbsp. chopped garlic
> salt and pepper to taste
> 1 large bunch cilantro, chopped
> 1/2 bunch parsley, chopped
> 1/2 tsp. aji pepper sauce or hot sauce

Combine all ingredients and mix well. Let marinate, refrigerated for at least three hours and up to 24 hours. Serve on a bed of leaf lettuce.

This dish is traditionally garnished with slices of cooked and chilled sweet potatoes and corn on the cob. An alternative choice is to serve it with cancha, a toasted Peruvian corn similar to corn nuts.

Cocktail Cameron

Chef Lawrence Gaddy

Serves 6

30 medium shrimp
5 plum tomatoes, diced
5 avocados, diced
½ bunch cilantro
1 lime
3 cups ketchup
¼ cup hot sauce
1 ½ cup orange juice
1 Spanish onion, diced
1 bay leaf
1 tsp. black peppercorns
1 lemon
6 cups water

Place water in a pot and bring to boil with bay leaf and peppercorns and a lemon cut in half. Place shrimp in water and cook for 3 to 4 minutes. Drain shrimp and cool in ice water.

In a bowl, add diced plum tomatoes, avocado, chopped cilantro, the juice of one lime, ketchup, onion, hot sauce and orange juice.

Stir all together and then add the shrimp.

Café on the Bay

2630 Harbourside Drive,
Longboat Key, FL
941-383-0440

Oyster Bienville

Keith Daum Cec

Serves 6

> 30 oysters on the half shell
> 6 strips of bacon
> 1/2 lb. cooked small shrimp
> 1/2 lb. crab meat
> 2 tbsp. butter
> 2 bunches green onions, chopped
> 4 tbsp. flour
> 2 cups heavy cream
> salt to taste
> Tabasco to taste

- In a large frying pan, cook bacon until crisp. Add butter to bacon fat to make a roux. Stir in flour over medium heat.

- When the flour blooms, slowly stir in cream. Stirring constantly until you have a thick cream sauce. Let cool slightly, if too thick add more cream. Add shrimp, crab and green onions to cream mixture.

- Season to taste with salt and Tabasco.

- Top oysters with cream sauce and bake in 350° oven until brown. This will take 15 – 20 minutes.

Mattison's Siesta Grill

1256 Old Stickney Point Road
Siesta Key, FL 34242
941-349-2800

Escargot with Shitake Mushrooms and Crusty Bread

Chef Dimitri Xinidis

Serves 2

1 package frozen escargot, rinsed in cold water
1/2 lb. Shitake mushrooms, cleaned and sliced
2 tbsp. chopped garlic
1/2 cup with wine
6 cherry tomatoes
3 tbsp. butter
olive oil
2 slices of French bread toasted and cut on the diagonal

Heat 2 medium sauté pans with canola oil. When oil begins to smoke, add shitake mushrooms and sauté for 1 minute.

Add escargot, garlic, shallots and salt and pepper.

Sauté until just heated through.

Deglaze pan with white wine, add cherry tomatoes and swirl in butter. Cook stirring constantly and remove from heat when sauce is well combined and sauce-like consistency.

To plate: Place bread on bottom of pasta bowl. Brush bread with olive oil and season lightly with salt and pepper. Pour escargot over top of one piece of bread and place second piece of bread on top.

Sangria Tapas Bar

1532 Main Street
Sarasota, FL 34236
941-956-TAPA

Solomillo Asado ala Sevillana
(Cold Roast Tenderloin Toast)

Chef Alex Amaro
Serves 16

Roast Tenderloin

> 2 lb. Tenderloin of beef
> 1/3 cup minced fresh garlic
> salt & pepper to taste

- Rub tenderloin with salt, pepper and garlic.
- Pre-heat oven to 350° and roast for 20 minutes or until tenderloin reaches 125° degrees (medium rare).
- When done place in a cooling rack.
- Slice tenderloin (thin slices).

Garnish

> 1 cup   red peppers brunoise*
> 1 cup   rellow peppers brunoise*
> 1 cup   red onion brunoise*
> 1 cup   parsley, chopped
> 1 cup   black olives, diced
> 1 cup   green olives, diced

- Set aside. Do not mix.

Sherry Vinaigrette

1 cup sherry wine vinegar
3 cups salad oil
1/4 cup Dijon mustard
1/4 cup garlic, minced
1 tsp. basil, dried
1 Tbsp. thyme, dried
1/3 cup balsamic vinegar
salt & pepper to taste

🍃 Place all ingredients in a bowl except the oil.

🍃 Mix all ingredients well. Whisk in the oil slowly.

🍃 Season with salt and pepper.

Assembly

🍃 Take 48 pieces of toast and top with thinly sliced tenderloin.

🍃 Sprinkle with the following ingredients one at a time:
green olives, red peppers, yellow peppers, red onions,
black olives and parsley.

🍃 Place some field greens on the center of a platter and arrange
the tenderloin toast.

🍃 Drizzle with sherry vinaigrette, salt and fresh ground pepper.

* Brunoise - confetti chop

Southgate Gourmet

2157 Siesta Drive
Sarasota, FL 34239
941-954-2280

Duck Confit

Chef Cliff Whatmore

Serves 4

1 duck quartered
1 cup salt
1 cup sugar
2 tbsp. poultry rub
2 cups carrots, diced
1 onion sliced, diced
1/4 cup red wine
1 cup rendered duck fat

🍂 Mix the salt and sugar together. Season the duck with the rub. Pack the duck in the salt/sugar mixture; making sure all duck is covered. Cure the duck overnight in this mixture.

🍂 Remove the duck from the salt and wipe off excess.

🍂 Brown the duck in a deep frying pan on high heat. Remove the duck when brown and pour off the fat into an empty can.

🪶 Place the carrots, onions, red wine, and ¾ cup of the duck fat that has cooled slightly into an oven roasting bag. Add the duck pieces and close bag tightly.

🪶 Cook in slow oven, 145° for 6 hours.

🪶 Remove from heat and let stand at room temperature for 15 minutes.

The versatile Confit can be reheated in the bag and served whole on the bone. Works well with the simplest to very rich accompaniments. If served whole, be very careful, as the duck is very tender. You may want to pull the meat off the bone and use the meat in a variety of applications such as: pasta, flat breads or even stews. It can be a great addition to a salad or a cheese plate. Especially good served with Apricot Vin, which can be found on the next page.

Dolphin Sculpture at City Island Park

Southgate Gourmet

2157 Siesta Drive
Sarasota, FL 34239
941-954-2280

Apricot Vin

Chef Cliff Whatmore

Use as a salad dressing or as a sauce for Duck Confit.

1 cup dried apricots, diced
2 tbsp. fennel seeds, blanched
1 tbsp. cumin or ajawian (Asian spice)
1/2 cup apple juice
1/4 cup rice wine vinegar
1/4 cup fish sauce
1/2 cup shallot, chopped
1/2 cup dried mango, diced
1 cup olive oil
1 tbsp. tamarind (spice)

- In a blender, mix ½ cup of the dried apricots and the spice with the juice, vinegar and fish sauce. Blend until smooth and oil is emulsified.
- Stir in the remaining dried fruit leaving them whole.

Pho Calli

1578 Main Street
Sarasota, FL 34236
941-955-2683

Spring Rolls

Serves 6

You will need to have on hand peanut sauce, rice paper wrappers, and filling ingredients prepared ahead of time. You can place all of the ingredients on the table and let guests make their own spring rolls, or make them and serve with peanut sauce.

> 1/2 lb. pork, thinly sliced strips
> 2 cups cooked, cleaned shrimp, cut in half lengthwise
> handful of fresh mint leaves mixed with lettuce
> 2 cups cooked vermicelli noodles

- Slide rice wrappers in water to moisten for 30 seconds.
- Place sliced pork across middle of wrapper.
- Place a layer of fresh shrimp along side of the pork.
- Top meat with vermicelli and mint/lettuce mixture.
- Fold rice wrapper up like an envelope.
- Serve with peanut sauce.

Peanut Sauce:

> 1 cup Hoisin sauce
> 1/2 cup peanut butter
> 1/4 cup sugar
> Dash of salt

- Mix above ingredients together in small bowl and set aside.

Word of Mouth

6604 Gateway Avenue
Sarasota, FL 34231
941-925-2400

Sweet Potato Pancake

Jeremy Adams

Serves 8

Pancake Batter:

2 sweet potatoes baked peeled and pureed
1 ½ cups all-purpose flour
1/4 cup sugar
2 tsp. baking powder
1 tsp. baking soda
3/4 tsp. salt
1 ½ cups low fat buttermilk
2 large eggs
3 tbsp. butter, melted
1/4 tsp. vanilla extract
1/2 tsp. ground cinnamon
1/2 tsp.3 ground cloves
1/2 tsp. nutmeg
1/2 tsp. allspice

Filling:

2 cups granola
1 chopped banana

🍃 Combine all the dry ingredients from above and sift into a large bowl.

🍃 In another bowl, lightly whisk the buttermilk, pureed sweet potato, melted butter and eggs.

🍃 Add the wet to the dry ingredients and whisk until blended.

🍃 Cover and chill for 1-4 hours.

🍃 Heat a large griddle and lightly brush with butter. Pour the batter using a ladle into the desired size pancake.

🍃 Place the granola and sliced banana on top of the mixture.

🍃 Cook about 3 minutes or until you see bubbles appearing and then turn and cook another 2-3 minutes.

🍃 Serve with banana side facing up with butter and maple syrup.

The Big Oak at Island Park

The Broken Egg

210 Avenida Madera
Siesta Key, FL 34242
941-346-2750

Potato Pancakes with Smoked Salmon and Dill Sour Cream

Holly Mosby

Serves 8 as an appetizer or 4 as an entrée

Dilled Sour Cream

¼ cup sour cream
3 tbsp. minced green onion
3 tbsp. fresh dill
2 tsp. lemon juice

🍃 Mix together and chill

Potato Pancakes

3 oz. thinly sliced smoked salmon
2 ½ cups shredded, peeled potatoes
1 egg, beaten
1/2 tsp salt and pepper
3 tbsp. minced green onion
butter for frying
flour for dredging
fresh dill for garnish

Mix potatoes, egg and salt and pepper. Dust in a little flour, just enough to tighten. Make silver dollar size patties or larger for entrée size.

Fry pancake in butter until brown on both sides. Keep warm in oven until service.

To serve, spread lightly with dilled sour cream and top with sliced salmon. Sprinkle a little fresh dill on top.

Fairy Sculpture in front of Florida Studio Theater

Word of Mouth

6604 Gateway Avenue
Sarasota, FL 34231
941-925-2400

Word of Mouth Granola

Donald Barry

Serves 8

8 cups rolled oats
4 cups whole wheat flakes
2 cups oat bran
2 cups steel cut oats
4 cups unsalted raw sunflower seeds
4 cups brown sugar
50 ounces apple juice
1/2 cup vanilla
1 cup Vermont maple syrup
Assorted dried apricots, raisins, almonds, dried cranberries,
     to taste

🍃 Combine the first six ingredients and add the
     apple juice, vanilla and syrup. Mix well.
🍃 Spread on a tray and bake at 350° turning every 10 minutes
     until crunchy.
🍃 When mixture is dry, add the assorted dried fruits and nuts.
🍃 Serve for breakfast with sliced fresh fruit on top.

Recipe may be easily cut.

The Broken Egg

210 Avenida Madera
Siesta Key, FL 34231
941-346-2750

Ham and Cheese Brunch Casserole

Holly Mosby

Serves 12

> 1 lb. bread cubes, crust removed, buttered
> 1 lb. choice of broccoli, onions, mushrooms, green peppers, asparagus tips, steamed
> 2 cups ham, cubed
> 3/4 cup shredded cheddar cheese
> 6 eggs
> 3 cups milk
> 2 tsp. dried onions
> 1/2 tsp. salt
> 1/2 tsp. dry mustard

Butter one side of bread. Put 1/3 of bread cubes, butter side up, in a 13 x 9 pan. Top with ham, cheese and vegetables. Repeat and end with bread.

Beat together eggs milk and seasonings. Pour over bread, cover and refrigerate overnight.

Bake uncovered at 325° for 50 minutes. Sprinkle with cheese and bake 10 minutes more.

Blue Dolphin Café

470 John Ringling Blvd.
St Armands Circle, FL 34238
941-388-3566

Upside Down French Toast

Makes 12 squares

1 stick of butter

1 cup brown sugar

20 oz. can chunked pineapple, drained (fresh is even better)

chopped nuts (optional)

2 medium size French bread loaves

4 eggs

2 cups half and half

1 tbsp. vanilla

🍃 Preheat oven to 350°

🍃 Melt butter in 9 x 12 pan, sprinkle with brown sugar and gently spread to cover bottom of pan. Sprinkle with pineapple and chopped nuts if desired.

🍃 Slice bread, (stale is best), on a diagonal, about one inch thick. Place bread snugly in a single layer over sugar, butter and pineapple layer. Mix eggs, cream, and vanilla to blend.

🍃 Pour over bread and cover. Refrigerate for at least 4 hours or over night.

Bake covered for 45 minutes at 350°, uncover and bake for 10 more minutes until set and firm.

While still very warm loosen sides from pan and invert onto platter, scraping any caramelized sugar and pineapple from bottom of pan to top of French toast.

Cut into 3 inch squares and serve garnished with powdered sugar.

Royal Palm on Palm Avenue

The Broken Egg

210 Avenida Madera
Siesta Key, FL 34242
941-346-2750

Brandied Apple Raisin Bread Pudding

Holly Mosby

Serves 12

1 cup dark brown sugar
1 tsp. cinnamon
1 tsp. nutmeg
1/2 cup dry white wine
1 oz. brandy
1 lb. day old French bread or cinnamon rolls
4 tart apples peeled and thinly sliced
1 cup raisins
1/2 cup slivered almonds
1 cup orange marmalade

- In a large bowl combine sugar, cinnamon, nutmeg, wine and brandy.

- Break bread into pieces and add to bowl. Mix in remaining ingredients.

- May be layered in a charlotte mold, or mixed all together and baked in a cake pan. Cover and bake at 325° for 1 hour.

- Serve warm with whipped cream.

Blue Dolphin Café

470 John Ringling Blvd.
St Armands Circle, FL 34238
941-388-3566

Blueberry & Raspberry Muffin Bake

Serves 8

1 cup frozen or fresh blueberries
1 cup frozen or fresh raspberries
6 cups cubed assorted muffins or quick breads
(stale is fine, I save left over muffins and heals of breads in freezer until I have enough).
5 eggs
2 cups half and half

Generously butter a large lasagna type pan. Toss berries and muffin cubes together in a bowl and spread out in pan, should be about 2-3 inches deep.

Combine eggs and cream to blend. Pour over muffin mixture and refrigerate for several hours or overnight. Cover and bake for 45 minutes at 350 degrees, uncover and bake about 10 minutes more until top and cake are firm to touch. Cut around edges of pan to loosen, cut into 2-inch squares, serving 2 or 3 per person.

Dust with powdered sugar, or for a spectacular presentation garnish with:

8 oz. softened cream cheese
3 Tbsp powdered sugar
2 tsp vanilla

Put into a squeeze bottle and squeeze out a lattice design on each serving.

41

Soups, Salads & Sides

Coconut Palm

43

Washingtonia palm at the Van Wezel

Morel Restaurant

3809 S. Tuttle Avenue
Sarasota, FL 34239
941-927-8716

Wild Mushroom Soup

Chef Fredy Mayer

Serves 4

1 medium shallot, finely chopped
1/2 clove of garlic, finely chopped
1 small onion
1 oz. olive oil
12 oz. wild mushrooms, (porccini, chanterelle, button, Portobello)
22 oz. chicken or vegetable stock
8 oz. heavy cream
juice of half a lemon
salt, nutmeg, pepper to taste
freshly chopped herbs; parsley, sage and thyme

🌿 Carefully "sweat," in a sauté pan the shallot, onion and garlic in the olive oil.

🌿 Add the finely chopped mushrooms and continue to sauté until the mushrooms have released their moisture.

🌿 Add the stock and allow to simmer for 3 to 4 minutes.

🌿 Blend the mixture to a chunky consistency. Bring to a boil.

🌿 Reduce heat and add the heavy cream. Season with salt, nutmeg, pepper, lemon juice and freshly chopped herbs.

🌿 Serve with a garnish of sautéed mushrooms and fresh herbs.

Ophelia's

9105 Midnight Pass Road
Siesta Key, FL 34242
(941) 349-2212

Roasted Roma Tomato and Pecorino Romano Soup

Chef Dan Olsen

Serves 8

12 Roma tomatoes
1/4 cup extra virgin olive oil
1 tbsp. chopped garlic
1 tbsp. chopped shallots
1 cup chicken stock
1 cup Marsala wine
1 qt. heavy whipping cream
8 fresh basil leaves, coarsely chopped
3/4 cup freshly grated Pecorino Romano cheese
salt and pepper to taste

Cut tomatoes in half lengthwise and place in a large mixing bowl. Add olive oil, garlic and shallots. Toss until evenly coated and season with salt and pepper.

Place tomatoes on a cookie sheet or large baking pan and place in a preheated 350° oven. Bake for approximately 25-30 minutes or until just browned on the edges. Remove from oven and let cool.

In a large saucepan or soup pot bring chicken stock, Marsala wine and heavy whipping cream just to a boil. Reduce heat and simmer. Add roasted tomatoes and continue to simmer for 30 to 40 minutes. Remove from heat and stir in Pecorino Romano and fresh basil.

With a blender, blend soup until completely smooth. Ladle soup through a fine mesh sieve into a container. Push the soup through the sieve with the ladle. Discard the solids. Season with salt and pepper until just right.

Serve with a few garlic croutons floating on the top.

For a more rustic feel to the soup, don't put the soup through the sieve. Substituting vegetable stock for chicken stock makes this a wonderful vegetarian soup.

Entrance to Harbor Acres Historic marker site of first Sarasota Post Office.

Madfish Grill

4059 Cattleman Road
Sarasota, FL 34233
941-377-3474

Jamaican Sweet Potato Bisque

Chef Lawrence C. Gaddy

Serves 8

2 lbs. sweet potatoes
1 large onion
4 stalks celery
1 tbsp. fresh ginger, grated
2 oz butter
1/2 tsp. tarragon
1/2 tsp cinnamon
1/2 tsp allspice
1 tsp. black pepper
1 tsp. salt
1 qt. water
1 qt. chicken stock
1 cup heavy cream

🍃 Peel and dice sweet potatoes, onions and celery.

🍃 Melt butter in a stockpot and add the potatoes, onion and celery. Sauté the vegetables until onions and celery are soft. Add grated ginger, tarragon, cinnamon and allspice.

🍃 Add chicken stock and water. Simmer until potatoes are tender. Season with salt and pepper.

🍃 Puree in a blender until completely smooth. Pour back into stockpot and add heavy cream.

Café Continental

5221 Ocean Blvd.
Siesta Key, FL 34242
941-346-3171

Tomato Rice Soup

Chef Christopher Hiering

Serves 8

1/2 cup cooked rice
1 large chopped red onion
1 grated carrot
1 finely chopped celery stalk
2 coarse chopped de-seeded tomatoes
2 cans vegetable stock
1 tbsp. brown sugar
1 tsp. black pepper
1/2 tsp. nutmeg
1/2 tsp. curry powder
1 large can tomato juice
1 pt. half and half

- Sauté onion, carrot, celery and tomatoes.

- Reduce vegetable stock and add sautéed ingredients.

- Season with sugar, pepper, nutmeg, and curry powder.

- Add tomato juice and half and half.

- Thicken with a roux. Roux is equal parts butter to flour. For this, use ½ stick butter to ½ cup flour. Mix together over heat until flour blooms and becomes fragrant. Add to soup stirring constantly.

Blasé Café

5263 Ocean Blvd.
Siesta Key, FL 34242
941-349-9822

Riviera Seafood Bisque

Chef Cynthia Breslin

Serves 4

2 tbsp. olive oil
2 cloves garlic, sliced thin
1 cup white wine
3 cups heavy cream
A good pinch of saffron
6 shrimp
6 scallops
1/3 cup crabmeat
10 grape tomatoes cut in half
1/2 cup baby spinach leaves
salt and pepper to taste
touch of Tabasco, optional

- In a medium pot, heat olive oil over medium heat and add sliced garlic and sauté until limp but not brown.

- Add white wine and reduce by half.

- Add heavy cream and saffron. Bring to a boil. Reduce heat and simmer for 5 to 7 minutes.

- Add shrimp and scallops and continue to simmer for 45 minutes.

- Add grape tomatoes and spinach along with salt and pepper.

- When spinach wilts add crabmeat and taste. Correct seasoning to your liking. Add Tabasco if desired and serve.

Bella Roma

5239 Ocean Blvd.
Siesta Key — Sarasota, FL 34242
941-349-0995

Zuppe di Pesce alle Laziale

Chef Flavio Cristofoli

Serves 4 to 8

> 1 small fillet of snapper
> 2 lobster tails
> 8 large shrimp
> 8 crab claws
> 8 mussels
> 8 oz. squid (optional)
> 1 clove garlic
> 1 pinch red peppers
> 1 small bunch fresh parsley, chopped
> 16 oz. fish stock or clam juice
> 6 oz. tomato sauce
> 1 glass white wine
> 1 loaf Italian bread
> salt and pepper

- Cut into fourths all the seafood listed above. In olive oil, sauté the garlic clove and the red pepper flakes.

- When garlic turns a golden color remove from heat and save.

- Coat bottom of large saucepan with olive oil. Put all seafood in the large saucepan. Sprinkle wine over seafood and add the tomato sauce, fish stock, parsley, salt and pepper.

- Cover and cook slowly over low heat for 15-20 minutes.

- Cut the Italian bread into 16 slices. Coat each slice with olive oil, garlic and salt and pepper. Bake in oven until bread is crispy. Put two slices of bread on each plate, cover with seafood.

The Bijou Café

1287 First Street
Sarasota, FL 34236
941-366-8111

Creamy Gazpacho Soup

Serves 6 to 8

> 4 very ripe tomatoes, peeled and seeded
> 1/2 can tomato puree
> 1 cucumber, peeled and seeded
> 1 red pepper
> 1 green pepper
> 1 small white onion
> 1 carrot
> 2 small cans V-8 juice or tomato juice
> 1 tbsp. virgin olive oil
> 1 tbsp. fresh garlic, chopped
> pinch of oregano, basil and thyme
> salt and pepper to taste
> dash of white Worcestershire sauce
> dash of Tabasco sauce
> 1/2 cup mayonnaise
> 1/2 cup sour cream

- Mix mayonnaise and sour cream together and refrigerate.
- Place all ingredients except the V-8 juice in a food processor and pulse to get a chunky, NOT pureed texture.
- Slowly add the V-8 juice until texture is to your liking.
- Chill thoroughly, preferably overnight, but at least 4 hours.
- Just before serving, blend the sour cream mixture into the Gazpacho with a wire whisk. If you prefer, you may also serve the sour cream mixture on the side and let guests add it to their own taste. Serve with fresh hot garlic bread.

The Ritz-Carlton, Vernona Restaurant, Sarasota

1111 Ritz Carlton Drive
Sarasota, FL 34236
941-309-2000

Chilled English Pea Soup with Stone Crab and Osetra Crème Fraiche

Chef Yves Vacheresse

Serves 10

> 3 lbs. organic English peas, shelled
> 4 cups heavy cream
> 2 cups chicken stock
> 1 lemon, juice only
> 10 stone crab claws
> Osetra caviar
> crème fraiche
> pea tendrils

🍃 Combine cream and stock in a medium saucepan. Season with sea salt and cayenne pepper. Bring to a boil. Add peas and cook for 10 minutes until peas are soft and vibrant green. Remove from heat. Transfer to a blender and puree until completely smooth. Add half of the lemon juice and check acidity. Add remaining juice if necessary. Adjust seasoning. Refrigerate for a minimum of two hours.

🍃 Whisk crème fraiche for a few seconds until consistency is loosened and creamy. Fold caviar delicately into cream. Reserve.

To serve: Spoon soup into 10 chilled soup bowls. Place meat of one crab claw in center of each bowl. Spoon crème fraiche next to crab. Arrange a pinch of pea tendrils to the side of crab. Spoon one-half teaspoon of caviar to complete garnish. Serve very cold. Enjoy!

Boar's Head Provisions Co., Inc.

400 Sarasota Quay
Sarasota, FL 34236
941-955-0994

Corn and Anjou Pear Salad

Corporate Executive Chef Eddy Ismail
Serves 3

> 4 ears of the sweetest corn you can find, (hybrid yellow & white is best)
> 4 tsp. extra virgin olive oil
> 6 slices Boar's Head naturally smoked sliced bacon
> 2 whole Anjou pears
> 6 oz. lemon-lime soda
> 1/3 tsp. kosher salt
> 1/4 tsp. freshly ground black pepper

🍃 Preheat oven to 400°. Cut corn into kernels, coat with olive oil and spread onto a large cookie sheet.

🍃 Roast corn in preheated oven for 15 minutes. Remove corn from oven and let cool.

🍃 In a sauté pan, sizzle bacon over medium heat until crispy. Drain bacon and set aside.

🍃 Soak pears in lemon-lime soda and lemon juice mixture for 5 minutes.

🍃 Drain pears and discard the liquid.

🍃 Crumble bacon into small pieces.

🍃 Mix corn, (with roasting oil), bacon, pears, salt and pepper. Toss well. Serve immediately.

The Ritz-Carlton, Golf Resort, Naples

2600 Tiburon Drive
Naples, FL 34109
239-539-2000

Tomato Mozzarella with Artichokes and Mixed Green Salad

Chef Massimo Veronesi Lemonia

Serves 2

2 medium Roma tomatoes, peeled and cut in quarters
2 tbsp. red wine vinaigrette
2 tbsp. extra-virgin olive oil
2 marinated artichokes
mixed green salad
1 tbsp. chopped chives
salt and pepper to taste
1 lb. buffalo mozzarella
2 sprigs baby arugula

- Peel Roma tomatoes and cut in quarters. Marinate the tomatoes with red wine vinaigrette, extra virgin olive oil, salt, pepper and chopped chives. Store in the fridge 1 to 2 hours.
- Cut the buffalo mozzarella into 6 slices.
- Cut artichoke into quarters.
- Arrange the tomato on the bottom of the plate with 3 slices of mozzarella on top.
- Toss the mixed green salad with balsamic vinaigrette and arrange on the center of the dish.
- Drizzle the mozzarella with a tablespoon of the juice of the tomato. Garnish with baby arugula.

55

Roy's Hawaiian Fusion

2000 Siesta Drive
Sarasota, FL 34239
941-952-0109

Waikola Salad with Romaine Lettuce, Avocado & Capers with a Creamy Parmesan Dressing

Serves 4

For the Salad:

2 heads of Romaine hearts cut into thick strips
1 avocado cut into segments
½ cup capers
¼ medium onion thinly shaved
1 tomato cut into pulp free strips
4 slices shaved Prosciutto ham

Creamy Parmesan Dressing:

1 cup mayonnaise
1 tbsp. Dijon mustard
1 tsp. hot sauce
1 tsp. fish sauce
1 tbsp. white wine vinegar
2 tsp. minced garlic
1 tsp. minced ginger
3 tbsp. thinly sliced chives
2 tbsp. shredded Parmesan cheese

Goat Cheese Crouton:

1 four oz log of goat cheese
1 egg, whisked
1 cup of flour
1 cup breadcrumbs
1 cup vegetable oil for browning the croutons

🍃 Preheat oven to 250°. In a mixing bowl, combine the ingredients for the Parmesan Dressing. Whisk to incorporate the ingredients fully. Take the four slices of Prosciutto and lay them flat on a baking sheet. Place the Prosciutto in the oven to slowly bake until crisp but not burned. This should take about 8 minutes. When the Prosciutto is crisp, remove from oven and let cool to room temperature.

🍃 For the goat cheese crouton, slice the goat cheese log into four medallions. Bread the goat cheese medallions by first coating them in flour then the egg and finally the breadcrumbs. Keep the croutons chilled in the refrigerator until you are ready to brown them in oil. Place the croutons into the oil in a medium skillet over medium high heat. Lightly brown on both sides. When the croutons are brown let them drain on a plate with a paper napkin.

🍃 To make the salads, make one salad at a time. Place one quarter of the romaine, shaved onion, and capers into a mixing bowl and toss with one fourth of the Parmesan dressing. Nicely pile the salad into the center of the chilled salad plate and garnish with the avocado slices, and tomato strips. Top with a goat cheese crouton and a Prosciutto crisp. Serve immediately.

"Death is inevitable, plan for it.
Life is brief so use it.
Heaven is real so invest in it."

—Author unknown

Whole Foods Market

1451 First Street
Sarasota, FL 34236
941-955-8500

Macadamia Crusted Goat Cheese Salad

Chef Mel Ruberg

Serves 2

> 1 lb. goat cheese
> 2 eggs beaten
> 1 bag baby field greens
> 1 lb fresh oyster mushrooms
> 1/2 lb. macadamia nuts ground
> 2 cloves garlic, chopped

🍃 Cut goat cheese into ½ inch pieces and freeze.

🍃 Dip frozen cheese into beaten egg and then roll in ground nuts.

🍃 Chop garlic and sauté in olive oil, add prepped mushrooms and cook until mushrooms are limp.

🍃 Place nut crusted goat cheese in oven for 15 minutes.

🍃 Arrange field greens on tray and scatter mushrooms then top with soft goat cheese.

Patrick's Restaurant

1400 Main Street
Sarasota, FL 34236
941-952-1170

Southwest Chicken Cobb Salad

Chef Robby Howlett
Serves 4

> 1 head of Romaine lettuce
> 2 boneless, skinless chicken breasts, grilled
> 1 cup roasted corn, (2 ears)
> 1 cup black beans, rinsed and drained
> 1 large tomato, diced
> 1 large cucumber, diced
> 1 cup red onion, small dice
> 2 cups shredded cheddar or manchengo cheese

Place bed of lettuce on each of four plates. Arrange ¼ cup of each of the corn, beans, tomato, cucumber and red onion in sections around the plate.

Place shredded cheese in the middle of the plate.

Slice the chicken breast in long narrow strips and place on top of the cheese. You want the chicken to be hot at this point so that it will slightly melt the cheese underneath.

Dressing:

Mix ½ cup Ranch dressing with ½ cup bottled Bar-B-Q sauce. Mix to combine and pour over salad. Avocado, Cilantro or even Ranch dressings work well as an alternative.

Hillview Grill

1920 Hillview Street
Sarasota, FL 34239
941-952-0045

Black Bean and Rice Salad

Miles and Mindy Millwee
Makes one and a half quarts

> 1 cup white rice
> 2 cups water
> 2 cups black beans and enough water to cover

Salad Mix:

> 1 red onion, diced fine
> 1 (14 oz.) can hearts of palm, diced ½ inch
> 1/2 cup roasted red peppers, well drained, diced fine
> 1 cup green olives, diced fine
> 3/4 cup red wine vinegar
> 2 tbsp. olive oil
> 1 tbsp. garlic
> 1 tbsp. cumin
> 1 tsp. salt
> 1 tbsp. black pepper

🌿 In two separate pots: cook rice and water in one, black beans in the other. Cover beans with water and cook until tender.

🌿 Drain off water and cool both rice and beans.

🌿 Combine all ingredients except hearts of palm, which are added last to maintain texture.

Chutney's Etc.

1944 Hillview Street
Sarasota, FL 34239
941-954-4444

Persian Chicken Salad

Denise May

Serves 8

4 boneless chicken breasts
3 hard boiled eggs, chopped fine
1 or 2 dill pickles, chopped fine
2 tsp. dill weed
1/2 cup green peas, thawed
mayonnaise to taste

Poach chicken in salt water, and then chop very fine.

Mix remaining ingredients in a bowl and add salt and pepper to taste. Serve on your favorite bread.

This recipe is well suited for a food processor to aid the chopping and mixing process.

"I'll be there for you.
I'll steal the sun from the sky for you.
I'll be there for you." — Aerosmith

61

Marjorie North

Feature writer for The Herald-Tribune

Tomato Pie

Makes one pie.

This is a great recipe and one you will want to try. Marjorie makes it at family gatherings and employs the kids to paint the piecrust with mustard and layer the tomatoes in and make the cheese crust. It is easy and fun for them and delicious to eat.

> 1 prepared frozen piecrust.
> 6 medium tomatoes, plum tomatoes work well
> Dijon mustard
> 1 lb. Monterey Jack cheese

🍃 Spread the mustard on bottom and sides of piecrust.

🍃 Thinly slice the tomatoes. If the tomatoes are very juicy let the juice run off.

🍃 Layer the tomatoes in the piecrust to fill the pie.

🍃 Layer the sliced cheese on top of the tomatoes creating a crust.

🍃 Bake in 350°. oven for 1 hour.

If the pie has plenty of liquid under the cheese pour the excess amount off. Let pie cool slightly before cutting. Enjoy!

Cru Bistro and Wine Bar

1377 Main Street
Sarasota, FL 34236
941-951-NAPA

Boniato Gnocchi

Chef Malin Parker

Serves 8

1 1/2 lb boniato, peeled (this is a Caribbean root and can be found in the produce section)
2 eggs
2 tsp. kosher salt
2 cups all purpose flour

🍃 Cook the boniato in salted water. Do not allow the water to boil hard, as the boniato will absorb too much water. When boniato is tender, grind or pass through a food mill or ricer.

🍃 Mix the boniato with eggs and the salt. Stir in the flour to make dough. Let dough rest for 1 hour.

🍃 Divide the dough into 6 parts.

🍃 Roll the dough into "ropes" about the size of your finger. Cut the "ropes" into ¾ " long pieces. Place on a floured sheet pan.

🍃 Once all the gnocchi has been formed, bring a pot of salted water to a boil. In batches add the gnocchi, cooking until the float. Remove from water with a slotted spoon and either serve at once or shock in ice water bath. If using later lightly oil the gnocchi and warm in oven to serve.

Notes from Chef Malin Parker:

Malin's good friend Darwin Santa Maria (owner of Selva Grill) turned him on to the boniato a few years ago when they were working together at Fred's. The boniato is extremely versatile. This is one really unique way to work with it. You can find the boniato at SweetBay and Save-A-Lot grocery stores or most Latin markets around Sarasota.

Fleming's Prime Steakhouse and Wine Bar

2001 Siesta Drive
Sarasota, FL 34239
941-358-9463

Fleming's Potatoes

Chef Russel Skall

Serves 6

> 1 ½ cups heavy cream
> 1 cup half and half
> 2 tsp. salt and pepper
> 1 small jalapeno pepper, minced
> 3 oz. chopped leeks
> 3 cups cheddar cheese, grated
> 4 lbs. potatoes

- Heat cream and half and half in a large saucepan on medium high heat. Bring to a simmer. Add salt and pepper.

- Finely dice the jalapeno pepper. Cut the ends off leeks and dice only the bottom 3" of leek into ½" dice. Place both in a large mixing bowl.

- When the cream is hot remove from heat, add cheddar cheese and blend in thoroughly.

- Peel potatoes and slice 1/4 " thick circles on a mandolin slicer. Combine potatoes and cream mixture in mixing bowl with leeks and jalapeno and stir to combine.

🍃 Spray sides and bottom of 9" x 12" baking pan with Pam. Place potato mixture in pan and evenly distribute the potatoes.

🍃 Cover with aluminum foil. Bake at 350°. for 35-45 minutes. Remove foil and bake an additional 10-15 minutes to brown top of potatoes.

Gillespie statue on upper Main.
Site of the first golf course in Sarasota

Cru Bistro and Wine Bar

1377 Main Street
Sarasota, FL 34236
941-951-NAPA

Mushroom Crespelle

Chef Chris Covelli

Serves 8

Crespelle Batter:
½ cup unbleached flour
2 large eggs
2 tbsp. chickpea flour
2 tbsp. unsalted butter, melted
¼ cup milk
salt and pepper to taste

Mushroom Filling:
½ lb. wild mushrooms, wild or fresh
2 cups ground beef
2 cloves garlic
1 medium onion, diced
salt and pepper to taste
4 tbsp. extra virgin olive oil

Mushroom Sauce:
2 cups heavy cream
½ cup of porcini mushrooms, chopped, (reserve hydrated
  porcini mushroom liquid)
¼ cup Italian white wine
2 cloves garlic
½ cup minced white onion
4 tbsp. extra virgin olive oil
1 tbsp. butter to finish

For the crepe batter:

✒ Place melted butter, eggs and mix in a bowl and whisk until well combined.

✒ Sift together chickpea and unbleached flour until completely combined and smooth with no lumps. Add salt and pepper to taste and let rest for ½ hour to one hour in the refrigerator.

For the sauce:

✒ In a medium saucepan, add extra virgin olive oil, garlic, and onion and cook for 5 minutes at a steady simmer.

✒ Add the chopped Porcini mushrooms and cook for 10 minutes on low steady simmer. Add the white wine and stir in to dissolve.

✒ Slowly whisk in the heavy cream in a steady stream. Bring mixture to a very low simmer. Add the butter to finish and continue to whisk even after removing the pan from the heat. This will prevent the creamy mixture from breaking.

For the filling:

✒ Heat a stainless steal pan and add the extra virgin olive oil, garlic and onion until you have a steady simmer.

✒ Add the ground beef and cook until it starts to brown, add mushrooms and cook until ground beef and mushrooms are at a desired consistency.

✒ Fill the crepes with mushroom filling and spoon sauce over the top and serve. Garnish with a dollop of sour cream or crème fraiche and few sliced mushrooms.

Marsha Fottler

Writes for Gulf Shore Life, Sarasota Magazine and many other publications.

Marilyn's Delmonico Potatoes

Serves 8

10 medium potatoes, peeled and cut into medium cubes

Cheese sauce:

6 tbsp. butter
6 tbsp. flour
2 cups milk
3/4 package of Cracker Barrel Vermont Cheddar Cheese,
    cut up or shredded
1 jar of Kraft Old English cheese
dash of salt and pepper and dry mustard
1 cup crushed Ritz crackers
extra pats of butter for topping

- Grease an oblong baking pan with Pam or butter.
- Boil the potatoes until soft, not mushy. Drain and set aside in a large mixing bowl.
- Blend butter and flour in a saucepan over medium heat. Add milk slowly. Add cheeses and blend until melted.
- Pour cheese over potatoes and add seasonings.
- Turn the potatoes into the greased baking pan and top with cracker crumbs and pats of butter.
- Bake uncovered at 350° for about 40 minutes, until bubbly and slightly brown.

Marsha hails from New Orleans and married a Bostonian providing an instant appreciation of New England style cooking. This recipe is from her sister-in-law, Marilyn, and is a favorite side dish for a casual buffet, potluck supper or served dinner. Recipe can be made a day ahead and reheated.

Harry's Continental Café

525 St. Jude's Drive
Longboat Key, FL 34228
941-383-0777

Mashed Rutabaga and Potatoes

Chef Harry Christiansen

Serves 4 - 6

> 1 large rutabaga peeled and cubed
> equal amount of potatoes peeled & cubed (same size as rutabaga)
> 1 stick unsalted butter
> salt and freshly ground pepper to taste
> ½ to 1 cup heavy cream
> just a hint of freshly ground nutmeg

✎ Starting with cold water, boil rutabaga and potatoes until fork tender. Rutabaga will take longer so start with it first and add potatoes when they are half cooked. Drain and put vegetables back in pot to steam out excess moisture on a very low heat for 30 seconds, don't scorch.

✎ Add butter, salt, pepper and mash.

✎ Add warmed cream a little at a time until you get the consistency you like. Add a hint of the fresh ground nutmeg.

Pasta

Senegal Palm

Photo Linda Thomas

71

*Tiki Sculpture at O'Leary's at Bay Front Park,
downtown Sarasota*

Uva Rara Ristorante

443 Burns Court
(Downtown) Sarasota, FL 34236
941-362-9006

Risotto Mare e Monti

Oscar Revelli di Beaumont

Serves 4

Marinade:

5 tbsp. butter	1 liter vegetable stock
3 tbsp. chopped red onions	3 oz. grated Parmigiano
2 cups Italian Arborio rice	12 jumbo shrimp
½ cup dry white wine	12 bay scallops

- Put 2 tbsp. of butter and 2 tbsp. of onion in a saucepan, cook over a gentle heat until soft and golden in color. Add the rice and cook, stirring continuously for 3 to 4 minutes. Sprinkle the wine, and as soon as it has evaporated add 1/2 cup of boiling stock.

- Continue cooking until liquid has been absorbed, then add more stock. Repeat this process until the rice has cooked for 15 minutes, adding smaller amounts of stock as the cooking progresses.

- Stir in the Parmigiano and season with salt and pepper to taste. The rice is ready when it has a little "bite" left in it. Turn off the heat, and then cover tightly for about 2 minutes to finish cooking with the remaining 3 tbsp. of butter.

- In a different pan, melt 1 tbsp. of butter with 1 tbsp. of onion. Add the shrimp and scallops. Cook until tender. Salt and pepper to taste. Now combine the seafood with the rice. The final touch, (optional)....shaved fresh white truffle.

Buena Appetito!

73

The Ritz-Carlton Gold Resort, Naples

3600 Tiburon Drive
Naples, FL 34109
239-593-2000

Ravioli with Ricotta & Spinach Butter Sage
Chef Massimo Veronesi Lemonia
Serves 8

For the pasta:
1 lb. all purpose flour
20 egg yolks
1 tbsp. olive oil
salt to taste

- Combine the egg yolks with olive oil and salt. Slowly incorporate the flour. If necessary, add some water. Add some flour if it is too thin. Rest the pasta in the fridge for 2-3 hours. Remove from the fridge and keep at room temperature for 30 minutes.

For the fillings:
14 oz. baby spinach
olive oil for sautéing
½ lb. ricotta cheese
2 egg yolks
salt and pepper to taste
pinch of nutmeg
zest of lemon
¼ lb. (4 oz.) Parmigiano-Reggiano cheese grated

- Saute the spinach in a hot pan with olive oil. Drain the excess water in a strainer and refrigerate. Chop the cooked spinach finely.

- Mix the spinach the ricotta cheese. Add the egg yolks, nutmeg, salt, pepper, lemon zest, and grated Parmigiano-Reggiano.

- Let the filling rest for 1 hour.

To assemble:

Roll the pasta at the last number on the pasta machine with semolina flour. Cut small squares and fill with spinach filling. Brush the ouside of the pasta with a little water. Let the ravioli dry for 1 hour. Cook in boiling water.

For the sauce:

    1 stick butter
    1 oz. fresh sage leaves
    3 tbsp. white wine
    zest of one lemon
    ¼ lb. Parmigiano-Reggiano cheese, grated

- Melt the butter with the sage leaves. Add white wine and lemon zest. Cook for a few minutes. Add the ravioli, and sauté until heated through.

- Serve on a family platter. Garnish with grated Parmigiano cheese.

Sculpture at Bay Front Park

Sean Beauchamp Brady

Italian cookbook author, Italian culinary tour guide & Sarasota resident.

Frittata di Spaghetti

Makes 1 omelet, serving 8 to 10

> 5 eggs
> ¼ cup grated Parmigiano - Reggiano, Pecorino-Romano or
>   Grana Padano cheese
> 3 oz. dried sausage, diced into ¼ " cubes
> ½ tsp. salt or to taste
> black pepper to taste
> 8 oz. spaghetti, cooked until firm (leftover & already sauced is ideal)
> 1 tbsp. olive oil
> 6 oz. mozzarella, diced into ¼ " cubes

In a large bowl, beat the eggs until well mixed. Add the grated cheese, the sausage, and spaghetti. Mix thoroughly, (a pasta fork works well for this). Season with the salt and a few grindings of pepper.

Add the oil to a 10-inch non-stick skillet. Place the pan over medium-low heat. Scoop half the eggs and the pasta mixture into the pan. Spread it out to the edges of the pan. Sprinkle the mozzarella evenly over the surface. Top with the remaining pasta and egg mixture.

Cook until the frittata is mostly set, about 8 minutes. The bottom will be lightly browned and there will be a bit of raw egg on the surface. Using a flexible, heat resistant spatula, loosen the edges and bottom of the frittata, and then slide it onto a plate, cooked side down. Place the pan over the plate and carefully flip the pan and plate to release the frittata back into the pan, uncooked side on the bottom. Continue cooking about 6 or more minutes until the underside is golden brown.

🍃 Allow to stand for 5 – 10 minutes, cut into wedges or squares using a serrated knife. Serve hot or at room temperature.

Wine suggestion: Serve with Aglianico, an Italian red wine grown in the Vesuvius area.

Chefs note: "Every time I head over to Italy, I dream of eating Cecilia's frittata di spaghetti. A true Baroness, and owner of two estates in the town of Pasetum, just south of Salerno, Cecilia Bellelli Baratta is always happy to whip up one of these for me using last night's spaghetti. I stand in the kitchen, a happy fool, nibbling this ingenious food, washing it down with a bottle of local wine".

She stands in traffic triangle in Harbor Acres neighborhood.

Café Amici

1371 Main Street - Downtown
Sarasota, FL 34236
941-951-6896

Fettuccine Amici

Chef Achille Nigri
Serves 8

1 lb. chicken breasts, cut into strips
1 quart heavy cream
1 bunch rosemary
4 cloves garlic
10 oz. parsley, chopped
1 lb. egg fettuccine
salt and pepper to taste
Parmesan cheese to taste
10 oz. sun dried tomatoes, soaked in hot water for 20 minutes,
   then chopped
10 oz. olive oil
1 tsp. butter

Grill the chicken with garlic, rosemary, parsley, oil, salt and pepper. Meanwhile cook the pasta al dente. In another pan, sauté the reconstituted sun dried tomatoes with butter.

Add the cream and ½ of the chicken cut into strips. Mix together with fettuccine and add the cheese, sprinkle with parsley and top with remaining chicken on plate and serve.

Michael's on East

1212 East Ave. S.
Sarasota, FL 34231
941-366-0007

Bowtie Pasta

Serves 4

>   olive oil for sautéing
>   4 oz Shitake mushrooms, sliced
>   4 oz pancetta, diced
>   4 tsp. garlic chopped
>   ½ cup julienne, sun-dried, tomato
>   1 lb. grilled boneless skinless chicken breasts, sliced
>   1 cup white wine
>   1 ½ cup heavy cream
>   4 oz. (1/2 cup) butter
>   1 cup grated Parmigiano cheese
>   1 cup julienne snow peas for garnish
>   salt and pepper to taste

- Bring pot of water to boil. Add bow tie pasta and cook according to package directions. While pasta is cooking make the sauce. Drain pasta when al dente and set aside while you finish the sauce.
- Put medium sauté pan on low to medium heat and add a little olive oil and pancetta. Cook until pancetta has released the fat.
- Add mushrooms, and garlic, sun-dried tomatoes cooking until mushrooms have cooked down and released their moisture.
- Add the chicken, white wine, and heavy cream stirring constantly to combine.
- Finish with butter and combine with pasta. Coat pasta with sauce and plate.
- Garnish with snow peas and grated Parmigiano cheese.

Ferrari's

4155 South Tamiami Trail
Sarasota, FL 34231
941-929-7900

Rigatoni Montanara

Francesco Mocci and Bruno Pasquali
Serves 6 to 8

2 lbs. Italian sausage
2 medium onions, sliced
3 green bell peppers, sliced
3 red bell peppers, sliced
3 cloves garlic, minced
1 tbsp. sugar
1 tsp. dried oregano leaves
1 tsp. dried basil leaves
1 tsp. dried thyme leaves
salt and black pepper
1 quart can crushed Italian plum tomatoes
1 lb. rigatoni pasta
chopped fresh parsley (optional)

Cut sausage into 1 inch pieces. Cook in large saucepan over medium-high heat until well browned. Remove sausage to paper towels; set aside.

Drain off all but ¼ cup drippings. Add all remaining ingredients except tomatoes, pasta and parsley to drippings. Cook and stir until vegetables are tender. Stir in reserved sausage and tomatoes with juice. Bring to a boil.

Reduce heat to low, simmer 45 minutes. Serve over hot pasta. Garnish with chopped parsley, if desired.

Turtle's Restaurant

8875 Midnight Pass Road
Siesta Key, FL 34242
941-346-2207

North Atlantic Salmon Pasta

John F. Hentshel

Serves one

> 8 oz. cubed salmon
> 1 pinch white pepper
> 1 tsp. roasted garlic
> 3 oz. champagne
> 2 oz. heavy cream
> 1 oz. fresh Parmesan cheese
> 4 oz. fresh spinach, chopped fine
> 8 oz. cooked linguini

Note: This dish moves very quickly. Total cooking time should be 3 minutes. Have all your ingredients ready to go before you start.

🍃 Prepare linguini according to package directions.

🍃 Sauté cubed salmon in olive oil until translucent.

🍃 Add white pepper and roasted garlic.

🍃 Deglaze the pan with champagne and add heavy cream, Parmesan cheese and spinach. Sauté for 1 minute.

🍃 Toss with linguini and serve.

J Ryan on the Grill

8389 South Tamiami Trail
Sarasota, FL 34231
941-923-3200

Portobello Mushroom with Salmon

Chef Christian Bousquet

Serves 8

2 lb. salmon cut into strips, (5 to a serving)
1 cup chopped, cooked bacon
3 heads portabello mushrooms, grilled and julienned
1 cup vodka
1 cup chopped fresh basil
1 pint heavy cream
1 lb. grated Parmesan cheese
3 lbs. cooked penne pasta

Sauté bacon with salmon and portabello mushroom. Add vodka, basil, cream and Parmesan cheese. Simmer for 2 minutes.

Add the penne pasta and toss for 2 minutes before serving.

"Greatness is not in where we stand, but in what direction we are moving. We must sail sometimes with the wind, sometimes against it — but sail we must, and not drift, nor lie at anchor."

Oliver Wendell Holmes

Caragiulo's Italian Restaurant

69 South Palm Avenue
Downtown Sarasota, FL 34236
941-951-0866

Linguine with White Clam Sauce

Grandma Caragiulo

Serves 4

4 tbsp. olive oil
1 large onion, finely chopped
3 garlic cloves, crushed
1 cup white wine
2 dozen little neck clams
1 jar or can (5 oz.) clams in natural juice (reserve juice)
12 oz. dried linguini
4 tbsp. finely chopped fresh flat leaf parsley
salt and fresh ground pepper to taste
6 oz. butter

🍃 Heat oil in a saucepan: add the onions and cook gently, stirring frequently for 5 minutes, until softened, but not brown.

🍃 Stir in the garlic, wine and reserve juice with salt to taste. Add a generous grinding of black pepper. Bring to a boil stirring, and then lower heat. Cover the pan and simmer the sauce gently for about 20 minutes, stirring occasionally.

🍃 Meanwhile, coil the linguine into a large saucepan of rapidly boiling salted water and cook for 10 – 12 minutes or until al dente.

🍃 Add fresh clams to simmering sauce and add butter. Simmer for 5 minutes in covered saucepan. Feel free to add additional fresh garlic to taste. When clams open, remove from heat. Do not overcook clams or they will get tough.

🍃 Drain linguine. Add finely chopped parsley to the sauce and season with salt and fresh pepper to taste. Pour drained pasta into saucepan and stir until pasta is evenly coated. Serve immediately and sprinkle with more parsley.

Do not add Parmesan cheese – my grandma will turn over!

Euphemia Haye Restaurant

5540 Gulf of Mexico Drive
Longboat Key, FL 34228
941-383-3633

Crispy Capellini Cake with Garlic Shrimp

Chef Raymond Arpke

Serves 4

6 oz. Capellini pasta (cooked al dente in salted water, and cooled
   or leftover pasta, preferably long such as spaghetti or linguini).
¼ cup red bell pepper cut in slivers
¼ cup green bell pepper cut in slivers
½ cup scallions, sliced
2 cups seasoned bread crumbs
3 tbsp. olive oil
6 tbsp. butter, soft
2 tbsp. Italian parsley, chopped
20 large shrimp, peeled and deveined with tails intact
4 large garlic cloves pressed
½ cup white wine
salt and pepper to taste

Take cooked pasta and form 4 rounds, 5 to 6 inches in
diameter, about ¾ to 1 inch thick. Press each round gently into
the seasoned breadcrumbs, coating each side evenly.

Heat 1 tsp. butter and 1 tsp olive oil in a 7 inch, non-stick fry
pan. Add ¼ of the red and green peppers, along with 1/8 of
the scallions. Place one of the rounds on top of the peppers
and onions, and sauté until brown. Turn and brown the other
side. Turn cake out onto a pan that will hold all four rounds
and keep them warm. Repeat with the 3 additional Capellini

rounds and keep warm until serving. You may make the cakes a day ahead. Refrigerate and reheat.

In a 10 to 12 inch sauté pan, heat the remaining olive oil, (2 ½ tbsp.), over high heat. Add the shrimp, the remaining scallions and garlic. Toss in the pan a few times and add the wine to deglaze the pan. When the wine comes to a boil, add the parsley and remaining soft butter. Shake pan constantly, until wine and butter thicken into a light sauce. Place 5 shrimp attractively on each Capellini cake and serve topped with the pan sauce.

At the corner of Main St. and Washington Blvd.

Fred's

1917 Osprey Avenue
Sarasota, FL 34239
941-364-5811

Basil Prawn and Feta Cavatappi Pasta

Chef Mario Martinez

Serves 4

2 tbsp. olive oil
1 yellow onion, diced
4 cloves garlic, minced
1 lb. prawns, peeled and de-veined
¼ cup Sauvignon Blanc wine, or other dry white wine
juice of ¼ lemon
5 Roma tomatoes, peeled and diced
¼ cup chopped fresh basil
2 tbsp. chopped fresh parsley
pinch of red pepper flakes
½ cup crumbled Feta cheese (Bulgarian is the best)
12 oz. cavatappi pasta, cooked al dente

- Heat olive oil in a skillet over medium-high heat. Briskly sauté the onion until softened, about 3 minutes.
- Add the garlic and prawns and cook just until prawns turn a bright orange color, about 5 minutes.
- Add wine, lemon juice and diced tomatoes, mixing thoroughly.
- When tomatoes have softened, add the basil, parsley and red pepper flakes.
- Cook for 2 minutes, and then fold in the Feta cheese. Heat until cheese has softened.
- Ladle the sauce over the prepared cavatappi.

Café L'Europe

431 Harding Circle
St. Armands Circle, FL 34236
941-388-4415

Fettuccini Robuchoun

Chef Jeff Trefrey
Serves 4

> 4 – 6 oz. lobster tails
> 1 lb. dry fettuccini
> 24 asparagus spears
> 2 shallots
> 2 cups white wine
> 1 cup heavy cream
> 1 stick butter
> 1 vanilla bean
> 1 tbsp. olive oil

- Poach lobster tails in boiling water for 5 minutes. Remove and cool in ice water. Remove meat from shell and cut into large chunks.

- Make a sauce by sautéing chopped shallots in olive oil until transparent.

- Add white wine and reduce by one half.

- Add heavy cream and again reduce volume by half. Cut vanilla bean in half lengthwise and scrape the moist seeds into cream mixture.

- Cut butter into 16 pieces. Remove pan from heat and whisk in butter. Keep pan in a warm place.

- Meanwhile, cook fettuccini in boiling salted water. When done, strain pasta to dry.

- To serve: place fettuccini in plate, top with lobster chunks and asparagus spears. Pour sauce over top. Serve immediately.

Fish
&
Seafood

Photo Linda Thomas

Foxtail Palm

Sign at O'Leary's at Bay Front Park

Hillview Grill

1920 Hillview Drive
Sarasota, FL 34239
941-952-0045

Grilled Fish with Island Salsa

Christine Earp

Island Fruit Salsa

Makes 4 - 5 cups of salsa, enough for 10 servings

> 2 cups vine ripe tomatoes peeled, seeded and diced ¼"
> 2 cups papaya, mango or melon peeled, diced ¼"
> 1 cup pineapple peeled, cored and diced ¼"
> 2 cups red onion, diced ¼"

Prepare all the above ingredients and place in a mixing bowl. Add 2 tbsp. of olive oil, 1 teaspoon ground cumin and 3 tbsp. fresh-chopped cilantro. Gently mix together all the above ingredients and let stand at least 1 hour before serving with grilled fish.

Fresh Grilled Fish

Figure 6 to 8 oz of fish per person. Select your favorite firm textured fish; Cobia, tuna or salmon will do well. For seasoning, mix equal parts salt, black pepper, red pepper and thyme. In a hurry, substitute Lawry's Seasoned Salt or Paul Prudhomme's Cajun Spice.

Lightly coat fish filets with olive oil. Grill should be very hot, just before grilling wipe a thin layer of olive oil on grill.

Place fish on grill for 2-4 minutes until clearly marked. Gently lift fish with a steel spatula and rotate ¼ turn. Grill 2-3 minutes, fish will be marked. Turn fish over and finish cooking. You might want to take fish off when slightly underdone for a moist fish.

Remove fish to platter and place in a warm 175-degree oven. Salsa may be placed on fish before finishing in oven, to let the flavors marinate the fish slightly or serve salsa on the side.

Mattison's Siesta Grille

1256 Old Stickney Point Road
Siesta Key - Sarasota, FL 34241
941-359-2800

Troutini

Chef Dimitri Xioudis
Serves 4 as appetizer or 2 as entrée

Buy or make ahead at least ½ cup basil pesto. Have on hand or make ahead lemon Buerre Blanc, recipe follows. Have ready small bottle of capers, rinsed and drained, chopped garlic and shallots, and 1 freshly diced large tomato. Bottle of white wine, opened. 1 bunch of fresh parsley Japanese bread crumbs, (panko) 2 medium trout filets 1 handful of alfalfa sprouts 2 handfuls of fresh spinach

Burre Blanc:

1 cup white wine, reduced to ¼ cup
¼ cup shallots diced
1 cup heavy cream
juice of 1 lemon

Simmer: over medium heat; watch and remove from heat when reduced by half.

- Spread a thin layer of basil pesto on the flesh side of trout and pat with panko bread crumbs. Sprinkle with salt and pepper.

- When ready to serve, heat a sauté pan with ¼ cup of canola oil to smoking point.

- Heat oven to 450°. Place trout in hot sauté pan skin side up for 1 minute. Turn over and sauté for 1 minute. Remove from pan and place in oven.

🍃 Throw two handfuls of spinach in hot sauté pan and cook until wilted. Add chopped garlic, salt and pepper and a splash of white wine to sauté pan and heat through.

To plate:

Place a small clump of alfalfa sprouts on plate. Place cooked spinach next to the sprouts. Take the trout out of the oven. Cut each filet into 5 or 6 pieces. Arrange the trout around spinach and sprouts. Sprinkle lightly with capers, chopped tomato and parsley. Pour lemon Buerre Blanc over trout and serve.

Fountain at the Mediterraneo Plaza at the top of Main Street

Beach Bistro

6600 Gulf Drive
Holmes Beach, FL 34217
941-778-6444

Floribbean Grouper with Red Pepper Papaya Jam

Chef Mac de Carl

Serves 4

> 4 – 8 oz portions of black grouper filets
> ¼ cup flour
> 2 eggs beaten with a splash of water
> 1 lb. of coconut shredded
> 1 lb. of cashew nuts, toasted

- In a 250° oven, toast coconut and cashews until golden brown. Pulse both in food processor to rough consistency.
- Season grouper with salt and pepper. Dredge one side of filet in flour, then egg wash and then coconut crust. The other side of filet is naked.
- Sauté crust side down in medium hot sauté pan with 3 tbsp. canola oil until light golden brown. Remove fish and drain oil from pan. Turn fish, sautéed side down and finish in a 350° oven for 8 to 10 minutes.

Red pepper papaya jam:

> 1 cup sugar
> 1 cup water
> 1 cup red wine vinegar
> 2 papayas
> 1 jalapeno pepper
> 4 medium red peppers

- Place all ingredients in a blender to puree. Heat in saucepan over medium high heat. Combine 2 tbsp. cornstarch with 2 tbsp water. Add to jam stirring constantly. Continue to stir until thick. Serve with grouper filets.

94

J Ryan on the Grill

8389 S. Tamiami Trail
Sarasota, FL 34231
941-923-3200

Grouper ala J Ryan

Chef Christian Bousquet

Serves 6

1 large head cabbage
6 – 7 oz. grouper portions
6 slices of ham
6 cups marinara sauce
2 cups white wine
Salt and pepper

🍃 Blanch large outside leaves of cabbage.

🍃 Saute grouper 1 minute on each side.

🍃 Wrap grouper first with a the slice of ham and then in the cabbage leaves.

🍃 Cover the bottom of baking pan with marinara sauce. Place grouper on top of sauce, and cover with more marinara sauce. Pour white wine over all.

🍃 Bake in 350° oven for 15 minutes.

Phillippi Creek Village Oyster Bar

5353 S. Tamiami Trail
Sarasota, FL 34231
941-926-4444

Grouper Provençal

Roy Lalone

Serves 4

4 – 5 oz portions of grouper
4 cups prepared rice of your choice
1 ½ lb small to medium shrimp
4 tbsp. chopped garlic
1 – 15 oz can pitted black olives
4 large chopped fresh tomatoes
1 cup sliced mushrooms
4 tbsp. butter

🍃 Grill grouper until fully cooked

🍃 Sauté butter, garlic, tomatoes, mushrooms and shrimp until heated through and shrimp are done.

🍃 Spread rice on dinner plate. Place grouper on top of bed of rice. Pour sauce over grouper and serve.

Blackened Red Snapper with Raisin Pecan Sauce

Steven Swenson

Serves 2

Buy one 5-7 ounce fillet of red snapper per person. Use your favorite Cajun or blackening seasoning. Easy, fast and delicious.

> 1/4 cup olive oil
> 1 large shallot chopped fine
> 1/2 cup pecan halves
> 1/2 cup white raisins
> 1/2 cup chicken stock
> 4 Tbsp. butter

🌿 Lightly coat both sides of two snapper fillets with blackening seasoning.

🌿 Cook fillets in a searing hot cast iron skillet until well done. Set aside.

🌿 In a separate skillet heat olive oil. Add shallot chopped fine, pecan halves and raisins (white if available). Cook for 1 minute and add ½ cup chicken stock. Reduce heat and slowly add butter stirring constantly until sauce thickens.

🌿 Pour sauce over fish and serve with your favorite vegetable & rice.

Greer's Grill

6566 Gateway Avenue
Sarasota, FL 34231
941-926-0606

Lemon Thyme Crusted Mangrove Snapper

Chef Jeff Yoakum

Serves 6

> 1 cup fresh breadcrumbs
> 1 tbsp dry thyme
> 2 tbsp lemon zest
> 2 tbsp dry parsley
> ¼ cup Grey Poupon mustard
> 6 snapper filets

🍃 Mix first 4 ingredients.

🍃 Brush each filet with mustard. Top with breadcrumb mixture.

🍃 Drizzle melted butter over each filet and bake at 450° for 5 – 7 minutes.

Senegal Palms at Van Wezel

Roy's Hawaiian Fusion

2000 Siesta Drive
Sarasota, FL 34239
941-952-0109

Roy's Wood Grilled Yellowtail Snapper with a Spicy Dynamite Aioli

Serves 4

> 4 six oz. filet of yellowtail snapper
> salt and pepper to taste
> 1 cup mayonnaise
> 1 tbsp. spicy chile pepper sesame oil
> 1 tbsp. togarashi
> 2 scallions bias cut
> 1 tbsp. soy sauce
> 1 tsp. fish sauce

Prepare for grilling. Preheat your oven broiler. You will want to grill the snapper over a medium to medium-high heat. While the grill is warming, combine the mayonnaise, spicy sesame oil, togarashi, scallion, soy sauce, and fish sauce in a mixing bowl.

Season the snapper with salt and pepper and oil the grill. Grill the snapper to medium rare. Remove the snapper and place on a baking sheet. Top each snapper filet with a quarter of the aioli and place the filets under the broiler. The snapper are done when they are just cooked through and the aioli is golden brown.

Madfish Grill

4059 Cattleman Road
Sarasota, FL 34233
941-377-3474

Snapper Voodoo

Chef Lawrence C. Gaddy

Serves 6

> 6 – 8 oz. pieces of snapper
> ½ cup vegetable oil
> 2 large onion, diced
> 2 stalks celery, diced
> 2 green peppers, diced
> 4 tbsp. flour
> ½ cup parsley
> 1 ½ tsp. allspice
> ½ tsp. thyme
> 2 bay leaves
> 1 tbsp. Worcestershire sauce
> 1 ½ tsp. Tabasco sauce
> 2 cloves garlic, crushed
> 1 ½ cup dry red wine
> 2 cups fish stock or chicken stock
> 4 large tomatoes, large diced

🌿 Heat ¼ cup of oil in sauté pan. Place fish in flour to dredge. Place fish in hot sauté pan. Cook for 3 minutes on each side or until brown. Pull off heat.

🌿 Place ¼ cup oil in saucepan and add onions, celery and peppers. Cook until tender. Add tomatoes, parsley, thyme, bay leaf, Worcestershire, Tabasco, garlic, red wine, allspice, and stock. Simmer 20 minutes.

🌿 Pour mixture over fish and bake in 350° oven for 15 minutes.

The Colony Resort

1620 Gulf of Mexico Dr.
Longboat Key, FL 34238
941-383-5558

The Colony Dining Room's Famous
Snapper Colony

Chef Roger Hopkins

Serves 4

2 lb. red or yellowtail snapper
8 oz. herbs of your choice, minced & mixed
4 oz. olive oil
1/2 cup rum, chef suggests Cruzan

Heat olive oil in heavy skillet pan, season snapper with herbs, skin side down. Cook the snapper until golden, turn, continue cooking another 5 minutes and flame with rum. Put in 350° oven for about 5 - 6 minutes.

Key Lime Beurre Blanc:

4 shallots, minced	1 lb. unsalted butter, cut into cubes
1 cup white wine	Salt and pepper to taste
1 oz. white vinegar	1 oz. key lime juice
4 oz. jumbo lump crabmeat	
4 oz sun dried tomatoes, cut julienne	
4 oz. fresh basil, chiffonade cut	

Simmer the shallots with wine and vinegar until reduced by half. Add butter and incorporate until fully emulsified. Season with salt and pepper. Add sun dried tomatoes, basil and crabmeat with a splash of key lime juice, stir and simmer. Place snapper on plate and spoon a generous amount of beurre blanc over the top. Garnish with fresh parsley.

Fleming's Steakhouse and Wine Bar

2001 Siesta Drive
Sarasota, FL 34232
941-358-9463

Charred Salmon

Chef Russell Skall

Serves 4

> 1 leek
> 3 stalks celery
> salt to taste
> Crisco oil for frying
> 2 lbs salmon
> 2 tsp. Cajun spice mix
> 4 tbsp butter
> fresh chopped parsley

🍃 Cut ends off leeks then cut into 4-3" sections. Cut into $1/8$ to $1/4$" julienne strips, wash, drain and place in mixing bowl.

🍃 Trim skin off celery and cut into 3" long by $1/8$ to $1/4$" wide julienne strips. Add to leeks in mixing bowl and sprinkle salt over vegetables and toss. Let sit for 10 minutes.

🍃 Fill a saucepan with Crisco oil and heat to 300°, cook vegetables until lightly golden and crispy, drain on paper towels and reserve.

🍃 Cut salmon in to 4 equal pieces. Sprinkle Cajun spice over top and bottom of salmon.

🍃 Melt butter in sauté pan set on medium high heat. Add salmon and cook to get a good char about 3-4 minutes each side.

🍃 Place salmon on a plate. Drizzle cabernet sauce on plate next to the salmon Garnish with vegetables and sprinkle with fresh parsley.

Cabernet Sauce

    1 tsp. butter melted
    1 Shallot
    Pinch of white pepper
    1 cup red wine
    1/3 cup chicken stock
    1/3 cup balsamic vinegar
    ½ lb salted butter

🍃 Place butter in saucepan over medium high heat.

🍃 Rough cut shallots, add white pepper and sauté for 4-5 minutes until golden.

🍃 Add red wine and balsamic vinegar reduce to half.

🍃 Add chicken stock and reduce again by half.

🍃 Cut butter into 1" pieces and slowly add to the sauce adding more butter as it melts. Continue until all butter is incorporated.

Jack Dowd's "Tourist at Art Center of Sarasota"

Simply Gourmet

4783 Swift Road
Sarasota, FL 34233
941-929-0066

Salmon Balsamico

Larry Barrett

Serves 4

Get the freshest possible salmon and the oldest Balsamic vinegar you can afford. For a large crowd serve the whole sides of the salmon roasted on a large cedar plank. It makes for a spectacular presentation. The salmon can be served warm or at room temperature.

> 4 – 6 oz salmon filets
> ½ tsp. salt
> ¼ tsp. fresh cracked black pepper
> clove of fresh garlic
> olive oil
> lemon slices

🍃 For the salmon, preheat oven to 450°. Wash and pat dry salmon. Make sure all pin bones are removed. Brush a sheet pan lightly with olive oil. Place salmon skin side down on pan. Cut clove of garlic in half and rub over fillet. Lightly dust with salt and pepper. Roast in oven for about 7 minutes until firm. Place under broiler to brown lightly for just a few seconds.

Balsamic Drizzle
> 1 cup two-year-old balsamic vinegar
> 3 tbsp. granulated sugar
> mixed baby lettuces

Balsamic drizzle: put vinegar and sugar in saucepan over medium high heat and reduce by half. It will get syrupy and coat the back of a spoon. Stir for about 10 minutes.

Place salmon fillet over a large mound of mixed baby lettuces. Drizzle vinegar reduction lightly over salmon with a spoon and garnish with chopped chives and lemon.

In front of Michael Saunders training facility - Osprey Avenue

Fleming's Steakhouse and Wine Bar

2001 Siesta Drive
Sarasota, FL 34232
941-358-9463

Orange Sesame Crusted Ahi Tuna

Chef Russell Skall

Serves 4

4 – 5 oz. portions of Ahi tuna medallions
5 tbsp. clarified butter
8 green onions

Ponzu sauce:

½ cup soy sauce
½ cup rice vinegar
4 tbsp. lemon juice
4 tbsp. lime juice
4 tbsp. pineapple juice
2 tbsp. pickled ginger
4 tsp. cilantro

✎ Combine all ingredients in saucepan and bring to a simmer for 8 to 10 minutes.

✎ Remove from heat and allow ginger to sit in pan for 5 minutes for the flavor to extract.

✎ Strain through a fine sieve and let cool.

Orange Sesame Crust:
8 large wonton shells
olive oil to cover bottom of fry pan
4 tbsp. white sesame seeds
4 tbsp. black sesame seeds
2 oranges

In a small saucepan heat oil to 300°. Fry wonton shells in oil until golden brown. Place in a mixing bowl and break apart into small pieces.

Lightly toast white sesame seed in 350° oven for 4 – 5 minutes until golden brown. Add black and toasted sesame seeds to bowl of broken wonton pieces.

Zest orange with no white parts and finely dice. Add to the bowl. Mix all ingredients well.

To assemble:
Season top and bottom of tuna medallions with orange sesame crust.

Put 1-tablespoon butter in sauté pan and sear tuna for 1 –2 minutes to lightly char.

Place fish on a small sheet pan and finish cooking in a 350° oven for 5-6 minutes.

Place sauce in center of hot fish plate and set tuna over the sauce.

Cut four green onions very thin on the bias 1" long. Brush the other 4 green onions with butter and cook under the broiler 45 seconds to wilt.

Lay broiled green onion over the top of fish and sprinkle cut pieces around the plate.

107

Pattigeorge

4120 Gulf of Mexico Drive
Longboat Key, FL 34228
941-383-5111

Ahi Tuna Tarter Wonton Tacos

Chef Tommy Klauber

Serves 4

Tuna:

> 1 lb sashimi grade Ahi tuna, finely diced
> ¼ tsp. sesame seeds, lightly toasted
> ½ tsp. fresh chopped ginger
> 1/8 cup soy sauce
> 1/8 cup sesame oil
> ¼ tsp. black sesame seeds
> 32 wonton wrappers

Place tuna, and all of the above ingredients except wonton wrappers in mixing bowl. Stir and let marinate for 5 minutes. Chill before using.

Sakimole: A creative twist on guacamole!

> 2 ripe avocados, peeled and pitted
> 1 medium tomato, peeled, seeded and small diced
> 1 jalapeno, seeded and minced
> 2 tbsp. onion, finely chopped
> 1 clove garlic, minced
> juice of 1 lemon
> juice of 1 lime
> 2 tbsp. cilantro, chopped
> 2 tbsp. Sake
> hot sauce to taste
> salt and pepper

🍃 In a mixing bowl, mash the avocados with a fork until they are somewhat mashed but still chunky. Fold in the remaining ingredients. Season with salt and pepper.

🍃 To store: cover tightly by layering a sheet of plastic wrap directly on the surface of the guacamole and gently squeezing out any air bubbles. Will keep up to 8 hours.

Assemble the wonton tacos:

🍃 Place wonton wrappers in folded- upright position (*I recommend using a specially designed holder for this*), fry tacos, until light brown and crispy then fill the wonton wrappers with guacamole and tuna.

🍃 Serve with Wasabi and fresh ginger.

Roy's Hawaiian Fusion

26831 South Bay Drive
Bonita Bay Promenade
Bonita Springs, FL 34134
239-489-7697

Roy's Seared Ahi
with Lilikoi-Shrimp Salsa

Serves 4

> 1 ripe passion fruit, halved
> 4 oz. extra large shrimp (about 4), peeled deveined & diced
> ½ tsp. olive oil
> ¼ cup minced Maui or other sweet onion
> 1 large Roma tomato, peeled, seeded, and finely diced
> 2 tbsp. scallions, finely diced, including green parts
> 1 tbsp. cilantro, minced
> 1 tsp. Tabasco sauce
> salt and freshly ground black pepper

🌿 Scoop the seeds and pulp from the passion fruit with a spoon and press through a fine-mesh sieve. Reserve the juice, (about 1 tablespoon) and discard the seeds and pulp.

🌿 Put the shrimp in a small bowl and toss with the olive oil to coat. Set a dry stainless steel sauté pan over high heat and when hot add the shrimp. Sear the shrimp turning often until evenly pink, about one minute.

🌿 Transfer to a plastic or glass bowl and add the reserved passion fruit juice, onion, tomato, scallion, cilantro, and Tabasco. Season with salt and pepper to taste.

🌿 Toss well to combine. Cover and refrigerate.

Put the Ahi on a plate, and coat with peanut oil. Season with salt and pepper to taste.

Set a dry cast iron skillet over high heat for 2 – 3 minutes. When pan is very hot sear the Ahi for about 30 seconds on each side for rare or about 1 ½ minutes on each side for medium-rare.

Transfer the Ahi to serving plates and spoon salsa over the tuna, letting the juices from the salsa run onto the plate.

On Palm Avenue in front of Ana Molinari Salon

Whole Foods Market

1451 First Street
Downtown Sarasota, FL 34236
941-955-8500

Herb Crusted Salmon on Cous Cous with Mixed Greens

Chef Mel Ruberg

Serves 2

> 1 lb. salmon
> 1 lb. cous cous
> 1 bag mixed greens
> ½ bunch of dill
> ½ bunch of mint
> 2 tbsp. olive oil
> 1 bottle Italian vinaigrette

🍃 Rough chop mint and dill and mix with olive oil.

🍃 Top the salmon with herb mixture and roast for 25 minutes at 350°.

🍃 Cook cous cous as per instructions on box while salmon is in the oven.

🍃 On each plate arrange greens on plate and top with cous cous. Place salmon on top of cous cous and pour vinaigrette over salmon, serve.

Bird Key Yacht Club

301 Bird Key Drive
Sarasota, FL 34236
941-953-4455

Seared Jumbo Scallops over Asparagus and Prosciutto Risotto

Chef Brent S. Williams

Serves 6

30 jumbo scallops 4 shallots minced
2 ½ cups Arborio rice
5 cups chicken stock — heat to simmer
1 large bunch asparagus — blanched
½ lb. Prosciutto diced

Tomato Fresca:

3 tomatoes peeled, seeded and diced
1/2 bunch cilantro minced
1/2 red onion diced
1 cup diced jicama
splash of lime juice
1 tbsp. olive oil
splash of balsamic vinegar

- Pan sear jumbo scallops until golden brown in olive oil. Set aside. Sauté shallots in a saucepot with olive oil until tender.
- Add rice and coat with oil.
- Slowly add stock over low to medium heat, stirring about 20 minutes or until all stock is absorbed (should be al dente and moist).
- Add blanched asparagus bias cut in half. Add the diced Prosciutto.
- Mix Tomato Fresca ingredients together in large bowl and chill for at least 1 hour.
- Serve the scallops over the risotto and top with Tomato Fresca.
- Garnish with fried, very thin yucca sticks if desired.

Fleming's Steakhouse and Wine Bar

2001 Siesta Drive
Sarasota, FL 34232
941-358-9463

Seared Curry Scallops wrapped in Bacon

Chef Russell Skall

Serves 4

20 large sea scallops	1 lb. blanched spinach
10 slices bacon	4 small Roma tomatoes, diced
4 tsp. curry powder	4 sprigs of tarragon
Salt and pepper to taste	4 tsp. chopped parsley
4 oz. clarified butter (half stick)	

- Remove side mussel from scallops if they are still in the shell.
- Cut bacon strips in half. Place on a sheet pan and cook in 350° oven for 4 – 5 minutes. Remove from oven and allow to cool. Wrap scallops with bacon and secure with toothpick or one 8" wood skewer, shish kabob style.
- Combine curry powder, salt and pepper and season top and bottom of each scallop. Place scallops on broiler pan and drizzle with butter. Cook scallops until golden brown in color – about 3 minutes per side for medium rare.
- If scallops need to be cooked longer place scallops on a metal sizzle plate and finish cooking in a 400° double convection oven set on high fan.
- Blanch the spinach and place spinach diagonally on the plate and set scallops on top of the spinach. Remove toothpicks or skewer.
- Ladle **Citrus Buerre Blanc** sauce over the scallops.
- Cut Roma tomatoes in fine dice and sprinkle over top of scallops. Garnish with tarragon sprig in center of plate. Last sprinkle 1 tbsp. of parsley over plate.

Citrus Buerre Blanc
Makes 1 cup

6 oz. butter, lightly salted
1 shallot
1 lime
1 orange
2 tbsp. fresh orange juice
2 tsp. lemon juice
2 tbsp. white wine
1 tbsp. heavy cream
2 tsp. sugar
½ tsp. kosher salt
2 tsp. fresh tarragon

- Melt 2 tbsp. butter in a saucepan set on medium heat and sauté minced shallots for 2 - 3 minutes.

- Segment the fruit and add with the juice from the fruit to the shallots. Set on medium high heat and cook for 2 - 3 minutes.

- Add orange and lemon juice to saucepan & cook to reduce slightly.

- Reduce heat to medium. Add white wine and simmer for another 2 - 3 minutes.

- Add cream, salt, sugar and minced tarragon, and reduce by half.

- Cut butter into 1" pieces and slowly add to reduction adding more butter as it melts in the sauce. Continue until all butter is incorporated.

Harry's Continental Kitchen

525 Saint Jude's Drive
Longboat Key, FL 34228
941-383-0777

Macadamia Nut Crusted Sea Scallops
with Mandarin Orange an Poppy Seed Butter

Serves 8

Butter Compote:
> 4 oz. soft butter
> 2 oz. frozen orange juice concentrate
> 2 oz. sugar
> 2 oz. poppy seeds
> dash of yellow food coloring

Nut Crust:
> 6 oz. macadamia nuts
> 2 oz. sugar
> 2 tsp. poppy seeds
> 1 whole orange rind grated

> 12 oz. Béchamel Sauce (see below)
> 15 oz. can fancy whole mandarin orange segments in light syrup
> 40 large sea scallops

- Whip all butter compote ingredients together. Chop all nut crust ingredients together. Place scallops on a cookie sheet. Roll scallop to coat in nut mixture.

- Bake in 425° oven for 10 minutes or until brown on top.

- Heat Béchamel and add butter compote with whisk.

- Puddle plate with bechemel sauce. Place 5 orange segments around on plate. Place scallops in between orange segments & serve.

Harry's Béchamel:

2 oz. soft butter
4 tsp. flour
2 cups half and half
salt and white pepper

🍃 Mix soft butter and flour together to make roux.

🍃 Stir over medium heat.

🍃 Add half and half. Add salt and pepper.

🍃 Bring to boil stirring constantly. Set aside.

Date Palms on Ringling Avenue

117

Javier's Restaurant & Wine Bar

6621 Midnight Pass Road
Siesta Key, FL 34242
941-349-1792

Conchitas á la Parmesana

Large sweet scallops quickly broiled with a crisp topping of lemon butter and Parmesan cheese. This dish is simplicity itself, but one that evokes fond memories of Peru for anyone who has traveled there. The briny, but sweet scallops are broiled until just tender with a light crust of Parmesan cheese. This dish, so popular in Peru, is truly representative of the cuisine of Peru's Pacific coast.

Proportions are not important, add more or less of something according to taste. Buy at least half a pound of scallops per person.

> large fresh sea scallops
> unsalted butter, cut into small pieces
> fresh squeezed lemon juice
> parmesan cheese
> scallop shells or broiler proof pan

✥ Place scallops in shell, top with butter and lemon juice and sprinkle generously with Parmesan cheese.

✥ Broil until top is brown and scallops are just cooked through.

Palm-lined Entrance to the Van Wezel Performing Arts Center

Mar Vista Dockside Restaurant and Pub

760 Broadway
Longboat Key, FL 34228
941-383-2391

Scallops Mar Vista

Chef Chris Buchan

Serves 5 - 6 (approximately 8 scallops per person)

> 3 oz. olive oil
> 40 fresh sea scallops
> 8 artichoke hearts, quartered
> 16 medium button mushrooms, quartered
> 6 oz. white wine
> 16 oz. garlic butter, (recipe follows)

Garlic Butter:

1 lb. salted butter	1/2 oz. Tabasco
1 ½ oz. chopped garlic	6 oz. fresh parsley, chopped
1 ½ oz. chopped shallots	1 oz. salt
1 oz. nutmeg	1/2 oz. white pepper
1 oz. Worcestershire sauce	

🍃 To make garlic butter. Soften butter, then add remaining ingredients and mix thoroughly.

🍃 Heat olive oil in large sauté pan. Just before the oil smokes add the scallops. Caramelize on both sides.

🍃 Add the mushrooms and sauté approximately 30 seconds. Add artichoke hearts.

🍃 Deglaze pan with white wine and reduce liquid to 2 oz or ¼ cup. Whisk in half of the garlic butter. Pull the pan off the heat and whisk in the remaining butter. Salt and pepper to taste. *Enjoy!!*

Roessler's Restaurant

2033 Vamo Way
South Sarasota, FL 34229
941-966-5688

Seared Sea Scallops with Romaine and White Truffle Sauce

Serves 4 - 6

1 ½ lbs. sea scallops
1 lb. Romaine lettuce
white truffle oil
salt and pepper

🌿 Heat skillet with canola oil. Lightly season scallops with kosher salt. Sear scallops in hot oil until golden. Turn and cook approximately 1 minute for large scallops.

For Sauce

🌿 Boil weak chicken stock, (chicken boullion will work fine). Drop clean romaine lettuce in stock and stir until wilted, about 1 minute. Remove lettuce and put into a blender with some of the stock. Blend well. You should have a green puree.

🌿 Add puree back into the stockpot and bring back to a boil. Season with 1 tbsp. cracked black pepper.

🌿 Strain stock and ladle into serving plates.

🌿 Place scallops on plate, drizzle with white truffle oil to taste and serve.

Dry Dock Waterfront Grill

412 Gulf of Mexico Drive
Longboat Key, FL 34238
941-383-0102

Shrimp Florentine

Tim Flynn
Makes 1 large or 2 small servings

6 large shrimp, cleaned and deveined
1 tsp. fresh thyme
¼ tsp. salt
¼ tsp. black pepper
1 tsp. fresh squeezed lemon juice
splash of Chablis wine
2 oz. fresh goat cheese
2 oz. baby spinach — cleaned, washed and **blanched**
4 tbsp. garlic butter
2 tbsp. herb bread crumbs

🍃 Place 6 shrimp in an oven proof baking dish.

🍃 Add thyme, salt, pepper, lemon juice and Chablis.

🍃 Broil in oven for approximately 10 minutes.

🍃 Add baby spinach, goat cheese, garlic butter and bread crumbs.

🍃 Broil in oven for 3 to 4 minutes until golden brown.

DeMarco's Italian Grill

3131 Clark Road
Sarasota, FL 34231
941-925-0226

Scampi Aioli

Chere DeMarco

Serves 4

The marriage of fresh garlic and olive oil in a critically acclaimed love story in which mild feta whispers sweet notions of tomatoes, olives, scallions and spinach in a union too good to be true!

16 large prawns or 20 medium shrimp
1/4 cup olive oil
4 garlic cloves, crushed
1/2 cup lemon juice
1/2 cup dry white wine
4 cups fresh spinach leaves
1/4 cup tomatoes, diced
1/4 cup black olives, sliced
1/2 cup feta cheese
1/8 cup scallions
salt and white pepper
1/8 cup asiago cheese

- Shell and clean scampi or shrimp. Wash under cold water and pat dry.
- Heat olive oil in sauté pan. Add shrimp and garlic and sauté over medium heat until shrimp is slightly pink.
- Squeeze lemon and add white wine. When wine is reduced by half add the spinach leaves, tomatoes, black olives, feta cheese and scallions. Season with salt and white pepper to taste. Sauté a few minutes longer and remove from heat.
- Place in a serving bowl and garnish with asiago cheese.

Beach Bistro

6600 Gulf Drive
Holmes Beach, FL 34217
941-778-6444

Famous Bistro Bouillabaisse

Chef Peter Arpke

This recipe gives you the foundation upon which to build a great Bouillabaisse. Purchase the appropriate amount of seafood to feed your guests. This is a recipe for the best base possible in order to make the most flavorful bouillabaisse.

Bouillabaisse Broth:

3 medium onions	2 large spoonfuls of tomato paste
3 leeks, white part only	1 large pinch of saffron threads
4 stalks of celery	3 tbsp. of shrimp or crab base
2 quarts clam juice	(if you have it, otherwise substitute chicken base)
1 quart tomato juice	2 tbsp. dried tarragon
1-quart tomatoes, diced	3 tbsp. fennel seed
2 cloves garlic. minced	dash of Tabasco sauce
2 cups white wine	1/4 cup of Pernod

Heat a heavy bottom stockpot over high heat. Add the oil and garlic. Sauté the garlic for 5 minutes and then add the celery, leeks and onions. Stir the vegetables well to prevent burning and allow to cook for an additional 3 to 4 minutes or until translucent. Add the bases, dried herbs, white wine and Pernod, bring to a simmer and allow to reduce for 5 minutes.

Add canned ingredients and bring to a boil, reduce heat and simmer for 10 minutes. Remove from heat and season to taste.

You now have an excellent broth in which to poach to order: sweet "Bubba" prawns, jumbo shrimp, premium market fish, shellfish and calamari. Chef recommends serving with clever sides of herbed garlic toast and aioli.

123

Javier's Restaurant & Wine Bar

6621 Midnight Pass Road
Siesta Key, FL 34242
941-349-1792

Arroz con Mariscos

Similar to seafood paella, an abundance of shrimp, scallops, fish, mussels and calamari saved with rice in a fresh ginger tomato sauce.

Serves 6

2 tbsp. olive oil	1/3 cup white wine
1 tbsp. garlic	1 bay leaf
2 cups chopped onions	2 cups chopped tomatoes
1 tsp. chopped ginger	Salt and pepper to taste
½ tsp. aji pepper or hot sauce	1 cup julienne red peppers
2 tsp. paprika	6 cups cooked rice
½ cup seafood stock	

☙ Sauté the garlic and onions in the olive oil until softened. Add the remaining ingredients except the red peppers and simmer until thickened and vegetables are tender.

☙ Add 2 –3 pounds of any combination of fresh seafood that is desired, (shrimp, scallops, clams, mussels, fish pieces or calamari). Add the red peppers and simmer until the seafood is just cooked through. Adjust seasonings and thoroughly mix in the rice.

☙ Garnish generously with chopped fresh cilantro.

The Colony Resort

1620 Gulf of Mexico Dr.
Longboat Key, FL 34238
941-383-5558

Fresh "Naked" Stone Crab Claws with Trio of Sauces

Chef Roger Hopkins

Makes one large appetizer serving

> 3 jumbo stone crab claws, cracked and cleaned of most shell
> 2 oz. stone crab knuckle meat (each claw will yield ½ - 1 oz of knuckle meat)
> ½ cup rum key lime mustard sauce (recipe follows)
> ½ cup classic cocktail sauce (recipe follows)
> 3 oz. mango—avacado—tomato Salsa (recipe follows)

For garnish:

> 1 large lemon, halved and hollowed
> 1 lime, quartered and marinated in rum
> fresh parsley

Special Equipment: chilled martini glasses

✒ Decorate martini glass by placing equal amounts of Key Lime mustard sauce and classic cocktail sauce side by side in martini glasses. Next, spoon a 3 oz. portion of mango- avocado-tomato salsa into lemon half.

✒ Place martini glass on plate. Arrange stone crab claws and knuckle meat on light bed of mixed greens on plate around martini glass. Garnish with a rum-marinated lime wedge, filled lemon half, and fresh parsley. Enjoy!

Rum Key Lime Mustard Sauce:
Makes about one cup

> 1/2 cup mayonnaise
> 1/4 cup Creole mustard
> 2 tbsp. Key lime juice
> 1 tbsp. cilantro, chopped
> 1/2 oz. rum

Classic Cocktail Sauce
Makes about 1 cup

> 1 cup ketchup
> 1 oz. (2 tbsp.) grated horseradish
> 1 tsp. hot sauce
> 2 tsp. Worcestershire sauce
> 1 tsp. lemon juice

Combine all ingredients. Adjust to taste.

Mango-Avocado-Tomato Salsa
Makes 2 cups

> 1 avocado, diced
> 1 mango, diced
> 1 tomato, diced
> 1 tbsp. red onion, diced
> 1 tbsp. red pepper, diced
> 1/2 tsp. cilantro, chopped
> 1/2 tsp. hot sauce (such as Tabasco)
> 1/2 tsp. Key limejuice
> 1/2 olive oil
> To taste salt and pepper

Mix all ingredients together and let sit for at least 1 hour.

Meat & Poultry

Bismark Palm
the Mac-Daddy of Palms

*Japanese Woman in garden at entrance
of Van Wezel Hall*

The Bean Stalk

2324 Gulf Gate Drive
Sarasota, FL 34231
941-927-3838

Wild Mushroom Meatloaf

Chef Heinz Claysen

4 lb. ground veal
1/4 lb. Crimini mushrooms
1/4 lb. oyster mushrooms
1/4 lb. shitake mushrooms
1/4 lb. button mushrooms
1/2 loaf Cuban bread cubed
1 large onion
1 pt. half and half
3 eggs
1/4 cup olive oil
1 tsp. thyme leaves
1/4 cup chicken base (granulated)
1 tsp. white pepper

Sauté mushrooms in oil and chicken base. Soak bread in half & half.

In bowl, combine ground veal, mushrooms, bread, eggs, and remaining ingredients and mix well.

Place mixture in meat loaf pan and bake in oven at 450° for 45 minutes. Remove from oven and let sit for 30 minutes.

Simply Gourmet

4783 Swift Road
Sarasota, FL 34231
941-929-0066

Beef Burgundy

Larry Barrett
Serves 4

3 slices bacon chopped	1 cup red burgundy wine
3 tbsp. butter	1 ½ cups rich beef or veal stock
1 lb. white button mushrooms	2 tbsp. chopped garlic
1 cup chopped onion	1 tsp. fresh thyme
2 lbs. sirloin cubed	pinch of basil
3 tbsp. flour	salt and black pepper

Heat a large deep braising pot over medium heat. Add bacon to pot and brown. Remove bacon bits and save for later. Add 1 ½ tbsp. butter to pot and melt with bacon drippings. Add mushrooms and cook for 5 minutes, add onions and cook until tender. Add salt and pepper to taste. Remove onions and mushrooms and keep warm.

Add remaining butter to pot, and then add meat and brown on all sides. Add flour to browned meat and cook for 2 minutes. Add garlic and cook 1 minute, stirring constantly. Add wine very slowly while stirring. When wine comes to a simmer, add stock and remaining herbs and spices. Cover the pot. When the liquid comes to a boil, reduce heat to medium. Cook covered for 20 minutes, add mushrooms, onions and bacon back to pot. Simmer with the cover off until sauce thickens a little. Adjust seasoning to taste.

Serve with wild rice pilaf, buttered noodles or potatoes of any kind.

Enchiladas Verdes

Bonifacio Caro

Serves 6

Salsa Verde:

1/2 onion cut in 3 pieces	1 avocado
10 jalapenos	1/2 oz. salt
3 fresh garlic cloves	10-15 corn tortillas
30 tomatillos	

✎ Boil the onion, jalapenos and tomatillos until jalapenos lose their green color. Cool.

✎ Mix together jalapenos, onions, tomatillos, avocado, garlic cloves, and salt and blend all.

Beef:

3 lbs. beef brisket
1/2 oz. black pepper
1/2 oz. salt
1/2 oz. garlic powder
3 cups water to cover

✎ Add all the ingredients and cook covered for 3 to 4 hours in a 350° oven, or you may cook in a crock-pot on low for 6-8 hours. Shred the beef when done. Add salsa and ricotta cheese if beef is dry

Lightly fry corn tortillas. Do not let them get hard. Roll the beef inside the tortillas and top with the Salsa Verde.

Morton's Market

1917 Osprey Avenue
Sarasota, FL 34239
941-364-5811

Cocoa Spice-Crusted Filet Mignon with Shrimp, Sweet Plantain Fufu and Chipolte Pepper Cream Sauce

Mario Martinez
Makes 6 servings

Sweet Plantain Fufu:

3 very ripe plantains (at least 75% black)
Vegetable oil for deep-frying
1/2 stick butter
2 Tbsp. Añejo (aged) rum
1 tsp. kosher salt
1/2 tsp. freshly ground pepper

Preheat frying oil to 350°. Peel and cut plantains into 1/2 inch-thick bias slices. Deep-fry the sliced sweet plantains in batches until well browned and caramelized on tips. Drain the fried plantain slices on paper towels and transfer to the bowl of a large food processor fitted with a metal blade. Pulse the plantains along with the remaining ingredients and then process only until it just forms a fairly smooth puree. Adjust seasoning and serve.

Chipotle Pepper Cream:

4 cups heavy cream, brought to a boil in a large heavy pot
    and reduced to 3 cups
1 tsp. kosher salt
1 Tbsp. pureed canned Chipotle peppers in adobo (available in
                                                Mexican markets)
1 Tbsp. tomato paste
Fresh lime juice to taste (optional)

🍃 Bring the reduced heavy cream to a boil in a medium saucepan,
taking care not to allow, "boil over". Reduce heat, add the
remaining ingredients, and simmer for 2 minutes. Strain
through a basket-strainer if desired. Fresh lime juice can be
added for acidity if desired.

Cocoa Spice Blend: Makes 1/2 cup

2 Tbsp. unsweetened cocoa   1 Tbsp. salt
1 Tbsp. light brown sugar   2 tsp. freshly ground pepper
1 tsp. chili powder   2 tsp. granulated garlic
2 tsp. granulated onion   1 tsp. ground cumin
1 tsp. ground allspice   1 tsp. Spanish paprika
1 tsp. ground thyme   1 tsp. ground coriander

🍃 Mix all ingredients until well blended.

Cocoa Spice-Crusted Filet Mignons & Flambéed Shrimp:

6 large shrimp or 12 medium shrimp, peeled and deveined
6 sugar cane skewers (5 inch long), cut to a point at one end
2 cups bottled Mojo Criollo marinade (available in Latin markets)
6 8–10 oz. Beef tenderloin filets
Cocoa spice blend
Salt and freshly ground pepper to taste
3 Tbsp. clarified butter
3 Tbsp. Anejo (aged) rum
2 Tbsp. finely minced chives
6 large sprigs of frisee

Skewer the shrimp on the sugar cane skewers and marinate in the Mojo Criollo for at least 4 hours or overnight. Totally encrust the 6 beef filets with the Cocoa spice blend and set aside.

Heat a large skillet over medium-high heat for 1-2 minutes. Drain the skewered shrimp and season with salt and pepper. Add the clarified butter to a pan, allowing it to get hot, but not smoking, and add the seasoned shrimp. Sauté the shrimp for 2-3 minutes, flambé with the rum, remove from heat, and toss in minced chives. Preheat broiler or charcoal grill to high heat. Broil or char-grill the filets to desired doneness.

Puddle six warmed plates with the Chipotle Cream Sauce and place a large scoop of the Sweet Plantain Fufu in each center. Lean the filet mignons on Fufu scoops, stick a skewered shrimp in the Fufu, garnish with the frisee sprig, and serve.

Ringling office building court yard

Roy's Hawaiian Fusion

26831 South Bay Drive
Bonita Bay Promenade
Bonita Springs, Florida 34134
239-489-7697

Roy's Baby Back Ribs

Serves 4 as an appetizer

> 2 lb. slab pork baby back ribs
> 2 tbsp. garlic powder
> 1 ½ tsp. ground white pepper
> 2 ½ tsp. Kosher salt
> ½ cup red wine
> ¾ cup butter, melted and cooked

🍃 Sprinkle ribs with garlic powder, pepper and salt. Place in a flat pan or sealable plastic bag. Add vinegar, coating the ribs well. Pour butter over ribs and mix well. Marinate 2 to 3 hours at room temperature.

🍃 Heat a covered charcoal or gas grill to medium heat and place ribs on the grill, meat side down. Cover and cook slowly, checking to be sure ribs do not burn. Baste with remaining marinade a few times. When ribs are nicely browned, turn.

🍃 Continue to cook, for a total of about 30 minutes. Remove ribs from grill, place on platter and cover with foil. Allow to rest 30 minutes before slicing into individual riblets and serving.

DeMarco's Italian Grill

3131 Clark Road
Sarasota, FL 34231
941-925-0226

Beef Brasato

Chere DeMarco

Serves 4

Amend our dining habits with this ceremonially grand dish of lean braised short ribs... Osso Bucco style with an unmistakably flavor of Bararolo wine.

 4 lean short ribs of beef
 ½ cup flour
 ¼ cup olive oil
 salt and black pepper
 ½ cup Barolo wine
 1 tbsp. fresh garlic
 1 medium onion, sliced
 2 tbsp. fresh parsley, chopped
 2 cups fresh tomato sauce
 ½ cup Parmesan cheese, freshly shredded

🍃 Coat short ribs with flour. Heat oil in sauté pan. Place short ribs in sauté pan and sear until brown on both sides. Season with salt and pepper to taste. Remove and place in baking pan without cover. Place in oven and braise about 40 minutes at 375°.

🍃 In a saucepan, combine fresh tomato sauce, wine, onion and parsley. Heat and simmer about 20 minutes longer. Remove from heat.

🍃 Pour sauce over short ribs and cover tightly. Bake in oven for 2 hours at 375°.

Oriental Food & Gift Mart

2234 Gulf Gate Drive
Sarasota, FL 34231
941-924-8066

Korean Short Ribs

Ko Cha Adam

Serves 4

> 1 lb. short ribs
> 3 tbsp. soy sauce
> 1 tbsp. sesame oil
> 1 tbsp. sugar
> 1 tsp. garlic
> 1 tsp. ginger
> 1 tbsp. minced white onion
> black pepper to taste

✎ Mix all ingredients together and marinate short ribs 30 minutes before cooking.

✎ Cook under broiler for 15 minutes. Will be slightly charred on the outside.

Marie's Italian Kitchen

5767 Beneva Road
Sarasota, FL 34233
941-923-1000

Citrus Braised Pork Shank with Bread Crumb Gremolata

Chef Bill Wells

Serves 4

6 pork shanks
1/2 cup olive oil
2 onions, chopped
2 carrots, chopped
2 celery ribs, chopped
6 cups chicken broth
2 lemons, zested
1/2 cup fresh bread crumbs
1/4 cup fresh flat-leaf parsley, chopped
2 lemons, juiced
salt and pepper
4 sprigs fresh thyme

🍃 Preheat oven to 350°. Season pork with salt and pepper. In ovenproof pot with lid, warm the oil. Add pork shanks (*you may roll the shanks in flour if you like*), brown well and remove.

🍃 Add the onion and carrot and sauté until they start to caramelize (*about 10 minutes*). Add the celery and thyme and sauté a few minutes more. Return the shanks to the pot, pour enough broth to cover the meat about 3/4 up the sides. Add half the zest and lemon juice and bring to a boil. Place covered in the oven to braise about 2 and half hours.

138

🍃 Prepare the breadcrumb mixture by warming a few teaspoons of oil in a small skillet and adding the bread crumbs, sautéing until they are brown. Add the lemon zest, parsley, and salt and pepper.

🍃 When the shanks are ready, they will be falling off the bone. Transfer to a platter. Cover and strain the cooking liquid. Return to heat and reduce to a thick sauce. Adjust the salt and pepper.

To serve pour the thickened sauce over the shanks and sprinkle the bread crumb mixture over all.

North end of First Street

Bella Roma

5239 Ocean Blvd.
Siesta Key, Florida 34242
941-349-0995

Osso Bucco alla Milanese

Flavio Cristofoli

Serves 4

4 veal shanks cut 3" thick	flour to dredge
2 oz. butter	1 fresh tomato, chopped (optional)
2 garlic cloves	Salt and pepper
1/2 large onion, chopped	
white wine (you may substitute chicken or beef broth)	

Gremolata sauce:

2 oz. fresh parsley	onion, chopped
zest of 1/2 lemon	2 anchovy filets, mashed
garlic, chopped	

In a large ovenproof pan, sauté garlic cloves and onion in 2 oz. of butter, when garlic cloves and onion are golden brown, remove and save. Brown the floured veal shanks on all sides in the pan. Reduce heat and cook slowly, sprinkling with white wine or broth and chopped tomato. Season with salt and pepper, and add garlic and onion back to the pan. Cover and cook in a 375° oven for 1 and 1/2 hours.

Prepare the gremolata sauce. Mix parsley, sautéed garlic, onion, and zest of lemon with mashed anchovy.

When veal shanks are done, spread Gremolata sauce on top of veal shanks and serve. This recipe is a classic and has been in the book since its inception.

Flavio suggests a nice bottle of Barberra wine to complement this dish.

Divino Restaurant

1766 Main Street
Sarasota, FL 34236
941-330-9393

Braised Veal Cheek with Porcini Mushrooms

Bozzolo Andres

Serves 6

1/2 bottle Nebbiolo* wine	1 onion, chopped
2 lbs. veal cheeks	4 tbsp. aged balsamic vinegar
2 oz. dried porcini mushrooms	salt and pepper, to taste
1 lb. porcini mushrooms, sliced	1 clove garlic, chopped
1 carrot, chopped	parsley
1 celery stalk, chopped	extra virgin olive oil

With a sharp knife, remove the fat from the veal cheeks. Season the veal cheeks with salt and pepper. Sauté veal cheeks in a pan in olive oil until brown. Drain veal in strainer to remove fat.

In a 350° oven, roast the carrot, celery and onion with a small amount of olive oil. When softened, add the veal, wine and allow the mixture to caramelize until the wine is completely evaporated. Add water and dried mushrooms to cover the meat. Add the balsamic vinegar and cover with aluminum foil. Cook for 1 and 1/4 hours at 350°. Remove the meat from the sauce and set aside. Reduce the sauce to the right consistency.

Sauté fresh porcini mushrooms and garlic in extra virgin olive oil until brown. Add to the sauce. Arrange veal cheeks on plates and spoon sauce over the meat. Garnish with chopped parsley.

* Italian red wine from Piedmont. Barollo or Barbaresco

Fred's

1917 Osprey Avenue
Sarasota, FL 34239
941-364-5811

Veal Scallops with Stone Crab Chunks, Mango & Island Spices

Mario Martinez

Serves 4
12 veal scallops (mini cutlets), pounded flat

Spiced Flour mixture:

1 cup flour
1 tbsp. salt
1 tsp. ground black pepper
1 tsp. granulated garlic
1 tsp. onion powder
1 tsp. curry powder
1/2 tsp. ground allspice
1/2 tsp. paprika

1/2 cup clarified butter

Sauté topping:

1/2 cup dry sherry (Tio Pepe, La Ina or comparable)
2 tbsp. fresh lemon juice
4 tbsp. butter, cut into 4 pats
1 cup diced ripe mango flesh
1 cup stone crab chunks (or other cooked & cleaned crab meat)
2 tbsp. mango Kuchela (available in west Indies markets)

Preheat oven to warm setting. In a large sauté pan, heat the clarified butter over medium high heat until a drop of water sizzles on it. Dredge the veal scallops through the spiced flour, shake off excess and lightly brown both sides of all 12 veal scallops. Transfer the scallops to a holding pan and keep warm in the oven.

Deglaze the pan with the sherry over the heat and reduce to medium low. Add butter, lemon juice and mango flesh and cook 2-3 minutes. Fold in stone crab chunks and mango Kuchela and cook until warmed. Arrange three scallops on each of four serving plates, spoon the sauté mixture over the veal and serve. Offer additional mango Kuchela as a condiment for those who may want more.

Sculpture in front of the Herald-Tribune office on Main Street

Café Baci

4001 S. Tamiami Trail
Sarasota, Florida 34233
941-921-4848

Veal Saltimbocca alla Romana

Joe Cirrintano

Serves 6

> 12 - 2 and 1/2 oz. veal scaloppini, pounded thin
> 12 thin slices Prosciutto
> 3 tbsp. fresh sage
> 1/2 cup dry Marsala wine
> 1 cup meat stock (demi-glaze) or beef bullion reduction
> 3 tbsp. heavy cream
> salt and pepper to taste
> 1 cup flour
> 1/4 cup olive oil
> 1/4 lb. butter

🌿 Lay scaloppini on plastic wrap on hard surface. Season lightly with salt and pepper. Sprinkle sage on 1 side of the veal to cover well. Cover sage with Prosciutto, gently pounding into veal with a meat tenderizer mallet. Lightly flour veal while oil is heating. Sauté with Prosciutto side down. Turn the veal and lightly cook on the other side.

🌿 Remove veal from pan and discard extra oil. Deglaze with Marsala wine and reduce liquid by half. Add demi-glaze, heavy cream, and salt and pepper to taste. Reduce sauce to 1/4 cup and add butter. Place veal on serving plate and top with sauce.

Maximo's

149 Avenida Messina
Siesta Key, FL 34242
941-346-7865

Veal Oscarina

Chef Massimiliano (Max)
Serves 4 generously

> 8   4 - 6 oz. pieces of veal (Pound very thin)
> 1 medium onion sliced thin
> 1/2 cup olive oil
> 1/2 tsp. sugar
> 1/3 cup balsamic vinegar
> 2/3 cup heavy whipping cream
> 2/3 cup white wine
> flour for dredging veal

🍃 To make the sauce: Heat sauté pan coated with olive oil on high heat. When very hot, stir onions until they start to brown and caramelize. Add balsamic vinegar, then heavy whipping cream and white wine. Simmer and season the sauce with salt and pepper.

🍃 Heat another sauté pan with olive oil. Coat veal with flour on both sides. Sear the veal quickly on both sides. Add the veal to the sauce so that it coats the veal. If the sauce is too thick, thin with wine.

🍃 Serve with pasta and grilled vegetables.

The Crow's Nest

Marina Restaurant & Tavern
1968 Tarpon Center Drive
Venice, Florida 34285
941-484-9551

Pan Seared Veal with Mushrooms over Gnocchi with Cambazola Bleu Cheese Sauce

Serves 4 people

- 4 - 4 oz. veal medallions (veal round is recommended)
- 20 morel mushrooms, sliced
- 1 tbsp. olive oil
- 2 tsp. chopped garlic
- 6 oz. Cambazola blue cheese (if unavailable, use Stilton or Gorgonzola)
- 6 oz. heavy cream
- 16 oz. potato gnocchi
- salt and pepper to taste
- chopped walnuts
- freshly grated Parmesan cheese

- Pound veal medallions until thin and cut each into 5 strips. Pan sear the veal strips in olive oil until browned. Add mushrooms and sauté lightly. Add chopped garlic. (*Do not brown*)

- In a saucepan, blend heavy cream and blue cheese and let thicken. Add already prepared potato gnocchi to sauce.

- Place gnocchi and sauce on plates and arrange veal medallions on top. Sprinkle with walnuts and freshly grated Parmesan cheese.

Enjoy with a nice Shiraz or Cabernet.

Ophelia's

9105 Midnight Pass Road
Siesta Key, FL 34242
941-349-2212

Pan Roasted New Zealand Lamb Rack with Pistachio Herb Goat Cheese Crust and Mint Infused Zinfandel Syrup

Dan Olsen

1 14-16 oz. lamb rack (Frenched)	1 tsp. fresh chopped parsley
2 tbsp. olive oil	1 bottle red zinfandel
3 oz. fresh goat cheese	1 cup granulated sugar
1 tbsp. chopped toasted pistachios	2 cups chopped fresh mint leaves
1 tsp. fresh chopped rosemary	1 tbsp. chopped shallot
1 tsp. fresh chopped thyme	salt and pepper to taste

For the pistachio herb goat cheese... in the mixing bowl, incorporate the goat cheese, pistachios, rosemary, thyme, basil, and parsley. Season with salt and pepper to taste.

For the mint infused zinfandel syrup...in medium saucepan whisk together sugar, zinfandel, shallots, and mint. Reduce over medium heat until a syrup consistency is reached. Syrup should coat the back of a spoon. Strain through fine mesh sieve and season with salt and pepper.

For the lamb, season lamb rack with salt and pepper. Heat olive oil over medium heat. Sear lamb meat side down for 5-6 minutes. Flip over and carefully spread pistachio herb goat cheeses evenly over the meat. Place lamb in 400° oven for 8-10 minutes or until medium rare. Allow meat to rest for 4-5 minutes before cutting. Drizzle with zinfandel syrup and serve with your preferred starch and/or vegetables.

Note: Medium Rare - Internal temperature 130°.
Rare - Internal temperature 120-125°.

Bijou Café

1287 First Street
Sarasota, Florida 34236
941-366-8111

Lamb Shank Braised in Zinfandel with Rosemary

Jean Pierre Knagg

Serves 4

3 tbsp. cooking oil
1/2 tsp. paprika
1/2 tsp. white pepper
1/4 tsp. cayenne powder
1/2 tsp. garlic powder
1 cup all-purpose flour
salt and fresh ground pepper to taste
4 lamb shanks, preferably fore-shanks
1/2 cup chopped celery
1/2 cup chopped yellow onion
1/4 cup chopped peeled carrot
5 cloves fresh garlic, peeled and coarsely chopped
4 cups red Zinfandel wine
fresh rosemary sprigs

Preheat oven to 350°. Heat the cooking oil in an ovenproof braising pan or casserole until medium hot. Mix paprika, white pepper, cayenne and garlic powder together and add to flour. Season shanks liberally with salt and black pepper. Dredge in seasoned flour and brown in oil, about 5 minutes per side.

✎ Remove shanks to a plate and keep warm. Reduce heat and add the chopped celery, onion, carrot, and garlic. Brown well, scraping the pan bottom occasionally so nothing burns. Carefully add the wine, then the shanks and rosemary sprigs. Add warm water to just cover the shanks. Bring to a boil on a stovetop. Cover tightly with aluminum foil and place in oven. Braise the shanks for about 2 hours or until the meat is almost falling off the bone.

✎ Can be served as is, or a sauce can be made, as follows: remove the fat floating on top of the liquid. Strain the braising liquid and puree the vegetables, then return the pureed vegetables to the cooking liquid. Bring to a boil and simmer until sauce reduces to about half and thickens. Season to taste and serve immediately. Serve with rice pilaf, risotto or hearty flavored mashed potatoes.

At the Entrance of the Van Wezel

Kay's Barbeque Restaurant and Catering Company

5445 North Washington
Sarasota, Florida 34239
941-355-5150

Chicken and Dumplings

Serves 4 - 6

- 1 - 3 to 5 lb. chicken cut in pieces
- 1/2 tsp. Lawry's seasoning salt
- 1/2 tsp. freshly ground pepper
- 1/8 tsp. ground nutmeg
- 1/8 tsp. ground basil
- 1/8 tsp. ground oregano
- 1/4 tsp. paprika
- all-purpose flour to dredge chicken
- 7 tbsp. olive oil or bacon drippings
- 1 medium onion, chopped
- 1 bell pepper, diced
- 1 celery stalk, chopped
- 2 carrots, chopped
- 2 bay leaves
- 6 – 8 cups of water
- 1 – 2 chicken bouillon cubes

For Dumplings:

- 1 1/4 cups all-purpose flour
- 1 1/2 tsp. baking powder
- 1 tsp. Lawry's seasoning salt
- 1 egg, beaten
- 1/2 cup buttermilk
- 1 tbsp. melted butter

Season chicken pieces with all of the spices above and dredge in flour. Heat 2 tbsp. oil or drippings in skillet and sauté chopped onion until golden. Remove onions from skillet and add the remaining 5 tbsp. of oil and fry chicken until golden brown.

Place pieces in large pot and add the browned onion, bell pepper, celery, carrots, bay leaves, water and bouillon. Bring to a boil, then reduce heat and let simmer for 30 minutes.

For the dumplings, sift together flour, baking powder and seasoning salt. Add beaten egg, melted butter and buttermilk and blend to form a soft, sticky ball of dough.

Use a regular spoon to drop 1 tbsp. of dough into stew at a time until all dough is gone. Cover pot for 20 minutes and let simmer. Dumplings will get puffy when done. Remove bay leaves and serve.

If you want to brown the dumplings, which is what Kay does, transfer to an oven-proof dish and place in 350° oven for 10 minutes.

Playing in the Rain Sculpture at the Sarasota Arts Center

Hillview Grill

1920 Hillview Street
Sarasota, FL 34239
941-952-0045

Cashew Chicken

Christine Earp
Serves 4

2 oz. oil	2 oz. sesame oil
1 cup sherry	4 oz. cashews
4 oz. Chinese BBQ sauce	3-4 cups broccoli florets
4 oz. soy sauce	16 oz. linguine
2 chicken breasts cut into bite size pieces	

Chinese BBQ sauce:

1 cup lite soy sauce	1 tsp ground ginger
1 oz. hot sauce	1 tsp. garlic powder
1/2 cup ketchup	1/2 cup honey

🍃 First make BBQ sauce by mixing all ingredients thoroughly.
Makes approximately 2 cups. Cook pasta.

🍃 Heat oil in large sauté pan to medium heat. Add chicken
chunks and sauté until nice and golden. Add sherry, Chinese
BBQ sauce, soy sauce, sesame oil, cashews and broccoli
florets, cooking for 2-3 minutes until broccoli is done. Add
cooked and drained pasta. Toss together, coating all pasta
with sauce. Pull pasta from pan with tongs.

🍃 Place pasta in bowl. Pour remaining ingredients over pasta and
serve family style.

The Bangkok Restaurant

4791 Swift Road
Sarasota, FL 34233
941-922-0703

Pineapple Curry Chicken

Poonthavee Doungnoi

Serves 6

- 4 cups coconut milk
- 3 tsp. sugar
- 4 tsp. fish sauce
- 4 tsp. red curry paste
- 2 cups pineapple chunks
- 3 pieces thinly chopped magrut leaves
- 3 cups chicken (24 oz.), chopped into bite size pieces

Simmer coconut milk in a pan. Add chicken, pineapple chunks, sugar, fish sauce, and magrut leaves.

Add red curry paste according to your taste. Cook until chicken is done and serve with rice.

A cynic is a man who knows the price of everything and the value of nothing.

—Oscar Wilde

153

Bird Key Yacht Club

301 Bird Key Drive
Sarasota, FL 34236
941-953-4455

Vezzole Chicken Portobello

Brent S. Williams
Serves 4

4 medium sized Portobello mushrooms
2 skinless boneless chicken breasts
1 bag fresh spinach
4 oz. feta cheese
splash balsamic vinegar

Tomato Basil Relish:

1 large tomato, chopped fine
2 tbsp. fresh basil, chopped
1 tbsp. olive oil
1 clove minced garlic

🌿 Combine above ingredients and set aside.

Veloute Sauce:

1/4 cup heavy cream
2 cups chicken stock, heated
3 oz. roux
salt & pepper

🌿 Make the roux using 2 tbsp. butter. Stir in 2 tbsp. flour.
When butter starts to turn golden and flour blooms, slowly
add chicken stock, stirring constantly. Add 1/4 cup heavy
cream and season with salt and pepper. Keep warm and
set aside.

Butterfly chicken breasts and pound thin. You should have 4 thin chicken breasts. Steam Portobello mushrooms 5 minutes and splash with balsamic vinegar. Sauté spinach with a dash of olive oil and a hint of garlic. Grill chicken and slice thin on the bias. Grill Portobello's.

Assemble mushroom, topped first with spinach. Add a layer of chicken, sprinkle on tomato relish and top with feta cheese. Broil 5 minutes until cheese browns slightly. Pour sauce over the top and serve.

Fish Sculpture at the Arts Center of Sarasota

Roy's Hawaiian Fusion

26831 South Bay Drive
Bonita Bay Promenade
Bonita Springs, Florida 34134
239-489-7697

Roy's Grilled Lemon Soy Garlic Butter Chicken

Chef Jamie

Serves 4

> 2 chicken halves, bone-in
> 8 oz. unsalted butter (melted in microwave for 15 seconds)
> 1/4 cup soy sauce
> 1/8 cup minced garlic
> 1/8 cup lemon juice
> salt & pepper
> 1 tbsp. minced ginger (optional)

✎ Mix all ingredients together and marinate chicken overnight.
Grill and enjoy.

Waterfront sculpture on the lawn at the Van Wezel

Desserts

Photo Linda Thomas

Royal Palm

Screw Pine

Amaretti Cookies

Larry Barrett

Easy and delicious!

8 oz. almond paste
1 cup sugar
2 large egg whites

Cut almond paste into 1/2 inch cubes, place in mixer. Add half the sugar and mix on low speed until the paste is broken into small crumbs. Add the rest of the sugar and continue to mix until the crumbs are very fine (about 2 minutes). Add the egg whites in 2 additions, scraping down the bowl. Make sure the batter is free of lumps. Don't overbeat.

Pipe cookies from a pastry bag with a 3/4 inch tip. Make each amaretti about 1 1/4 inches in diameter and 1/2 inch high; leave about 1 1/2 inches between cookies. You can scoop amaretti about 1 tsp. full per cookie.

Wet cotton cloth-just damp. Pat top of cookies to smooth and help to promote cracking during baking. Sprinkle with sugar. Bake at 350° about 15 minutes, until well raised and covered with fine cracks.

Ruth Landou

Freelance writer seen regularly in Style magazine, in the Herald-Tribune and other regional publications and communications. Officer for the Community Foundation of Sarasota County

Prosecco and Summer Fruit Terrine

Serves 8

Time to make: 15 minutes. Must chill for at least 8 hours.

From my husband Michael who got it from Gourmet magazine, August 2002. It is yummy and simple and you can vary the fruits, as you like. Delicious served with shortbread cookies. People are very impressed when they see it because it looks like something they'd serve in Lutece or some other fancy schmancy New York restaurant! The colors of the fruit are vivid and the Prosecco is clear as glass. – Ruth Landou

4 cups mixed fruit such as raspberries, strawberries and blueberries. Can use frozen fruit, which is defrosted and drained in a colander; also halved, seedless green grapes. If you use fresh peaches or nectarines, they should be blanched, peeled and thinly sliced.

2 ¾ tsp. unflavored gelatin (from two ¼ oz envelopes)
2 cups Prosecco (Italian sparkling white wine)
½ cups sugar
2 tsp. fresh lemon juice

🍃 Arrange fruit in a 1 ½ quart glass, or ceramic or nonstick terrine or loaf pan.

🍃 Sprinkle gelatin over ¼ cup Prosecco in a small bowl and let stand 1 minute to soften. Bring 1 cup Prosecco to a boil in a pan with sugar, stirring until sugar is dissolved. Remove from heat and add gelatin mixture, stirring until dissolved. Stir in remaining ¾ cup Prosecco and lemon juice, then transfer to a metal bowl set in larger bowl of ice and cold water. Cool mixture, stirring occasionally, just to room temperature.

Slowly pour mixture over fruit then chill, covered until firm, for at least 6 hours.

To unmold, dip pan in a larger pan of hot water for 3 to 5 seconds to loosen. Invert a serving plate over the terrine and plop the contents out.

Terrine may chill for up to 3 days. Unmold just before serving.

View of Bayfront from O'Leary's

Boar's Head Provision Co.

400 Sarasota Quay
Sarasota, FL 34236
941-955-0994

Apple Streusel

Eddy Ismail

Serves 6 - 8

> 8 Granny Smith apples
> 1 cup water
> 1 ½ cups dark brown sugar (loose pack)
> 1/4 cup granulated sugar
> 1/2 tsp. ground cinnamon
> 1/8 tsp. ground allspice
> 1/2 tsp. fresh ginger root, peeled and finely minced

Slurry

> 3 tbsp. water
> 1/3 cup cornstarch

Streusel Topping

> 1/4 lb. unsalted European-style butter (such as Plugra)
> 2 cups all-purpose flour
> 1 ½ cups light brown sugar (loose pack)
> 1 tsp. ground cinnamon
> 1/2 tsp. ground allspice
> 1 tsp. Kosher salt

Preheat oven to 350°. Prepare streusel topping by whipping butter in a cake mixer until soft. Add the rest of the struesel ingredients and mix on medium speed until mealy. Set streussel topping aside and keep in a cool place.

Peel and core apples, cut into 8 wedges and soak in water with some lemon juice to prevent from turning brown.

In a tall saucepot, combine water, dark brown sugar, granulated sugar, cinnamon, allspice and ginger and bring to a boil over medium heat.

Add slurry and keep on stirring until thickened. Pull away from heat.

Drain apples, add to sugar mixture and mix well. Place in a 14" x 12" x 2½" pan.

Spread streusel mix over apples. Bake for 45 to 50 minutes. Best served hot with home-made vanilla bean ice cream.

O'Leary's Bayfront

Harry's Continental Kitchen

525 St. Jude's Drive
Longboat Key, FL 34228
941-383-0777

Peanut Butter Pie

Chef Harry Christiensen
Serves 8

Pie Filling

1 cooked pie shell
4 eggs
1/2 tsp. cream of tartar
1/2 lb. butter
2 cups powdered sugar
2 ½ tsp. vanilla
10 oz. peanut butter

Chocolate Topping

4 oz. semi sweet chocolate
2 oz. unsweetened chocolate
1/4 cup coffee
1 tbsp. sugar
handful of unsalted peanuts,
        chopped

- Separate egg yolks and set aside.

- Whip eggs whites with cream of tartar until they peak. Set aside for later.

- Whip butter until creamy adding sugar, vanilla and peanut butter. When mixture is creamy, gradually add egg yolks until well blended. Take this mixture and fold into the egg whites.

- Fill cooked pie shell and refrigerate.

- Prepare chocolate topping and keep at room temperature.

- After refrigerating pie for one hour, cover with chocolate topping and sprinkle with chopped unsalted peanuts. Keep refrigerated until ready to serve.

164

Beach Bistro

6600 Gulf Drive
Holmes Beach, FL 34218
941-778-6444

Bananas Foster

Chef Peter Arpke

A classic! Bananas flamed with rum, banana liqueur and cinnamon sugar. Served with French vanilla ice cream. Makes a great visual presentation.

Serves 6

> 3 large bananas sliced
> 1/4 lb. butter, unsalted
> 6 tbsp. light brown sugar
> 2 tbsp. cinnamon sugar mixture
> 2 oz. Crème de Banana liqueur
> 1 oz. 151 rum
> vanilla ice cream

- Over medium heat melt butter and dissolve brown sugar with banana liqueur until smooth.

- Add bananas and coat. Gather mixture to one end of the pan while heating the other side of the pan, pull from flame (important) and add 151 rum. Ignite rum.

- Sprinkle cinnamon/sugar mixture into the flame, coming in low and from the side. Be careful not to over cook the bananas.

- Serve with vanilla ice cream.

Marie's Italian Kitchen

5767 Beneva Road
Sarasota, FL 34233
941-923-1000

Ilona Torte

Bill Wells

Serves 8

2 cups sugar
½ cup water
10 oz. semisweet chocolate cut in bits
12 tbsp. butter, room temperature
16 eggs, separated
3 ½ cups walnuts, coarsely ground
4 tbsp. fresh white breadcrumbs
pinch of salt

 Preheat oven to 375°. Butter 10" spring form pan. Cut round wax paper to fit bottom of pan. Flour the pan and shake out excess flour.

 Combine 2 cups sugar and ½ cup water in saucepan; simmer 5 minutes to make syrup. Add to syrup 10 oz. chocolate. Remove from heat, stir to melt, set aside, let cool.

 In mixer, beat 12 tbsp. butter until soft. Add 16 egg yolks one at a time on low speed. Add 1/2 chocolate mixture, and then add 3 ½ cups of ground walnuts, then the remaining syrup and 4 tbsp. breadcrumbs.

 In a large bowl, beat 16 egg whites with a pinch of salt until stiff peaks form. Stir 1/3 of the egg white mixture into the chocolate then add this lightened mixture into the whites blending but not deflating.

Pour the batter into the spring form pan. Bake for 35 to 40 minutes until set but will still feel spongy in the center.

Cool in pan for 15 minutes then run knife around sides. Invert onto rack and let cool completely – 2 hours before frosting.

Butter cream

12 oz. semisweet chocolate chips
2/3 cup water
4 tsp. instant espresso powder
2-1/2 cups butter, room temperature
6 egg yolks
1-1/2 cups confectioners' sugar
2/3 cup walnuts, ground

Combine 12 oz. chocolate, 2/3 cup water, and 4 tps. Espresso powder. Stir over low heat until melted, then cool completely.

Using an electric beater, cream butter, and 6 egg yolks one at a time. Slowly add 1 ½ cups confectioners sugar, blend thoroughly. Split the cake in half horizontally, reserve 1 cup of frosting for decorating, and cover the cake with frosting. Sprinkle with nuts to garnish.

Zoria

1991 Main Street
Sarasota, FL 34236
941-955-4457

Fresh Fruit Cobbler

Arthur Lopes, Pastry Chef & Proprietor

Topping
4 cups flour
1 lb. butter, unsalted
8 tbsp. sugar
6 tbsp. milk

Fruit Filling
8 - 10 cups fresh fruit
1/3 cup flour
1/4 cup corn starch
1 ½ cup sugar

Cut cold butter into cubes. With your hands, mix butter, flour
and sugar until ingredients come together. Add milk and toss.
Do not over mix.

For the filling, cut fruit and mix with flour, starch and sugar. Put
fruit mixture into a 10" x 15" baking dish. Sprinkle crumb
topping over top of fruit. Dust top with sugar.

Bake at 350° for 40 – 50 minutes.

2236 Gulf Gate Drive
Sarasota, FL 34231
941-927-2612

Lavender Pound Cake

Sandra Cherry, Former Owner

Makes one pound cake

2 1/2 cups all purpose flour
2 cups sugar
1/2 tsp. salt
1/2 tsp. soda
3 eggs
1 cup butter
1   8 oz. carton lemon yogurt
2 tbsp. pure lavender heads (make sure it is pure, no additions)

🌿 Combine all ingredients in large bowl, blend at low speed, and then beat 3 – 4 minutes at medium speed.

🌿 Pour into greased bundt pan and bake at 325° for 55 – 60 minutes. Test with a cake tester or toothpick to make sure that it is done.

🌿 Cool in pan about 20 minutes before inverting onto cooling rack.

🌿 Can be glazed with confectioner's sugar, milk and lemon juice.

The Crow's Nest

1968 Tarpon Center Drive
Venice, FL 34293
941-484-9551

Crème au Caramel

Serves 8

Custard

> 3/4 quart whole milk
> 6 eggs
> 5 oz. granulated sugar
> 2 dashes vanilla

🍃 Mix all together, strain and skim any foam from top.

Caramel

> 5 oz. granulated sugar
> 1 tbsp. water
> 1 oz. lemon juice

🍃 In a small saucepan, on medium- low heat, caramelize sugar to a rich caramel color.

🍃 Spoon 2 tablespoons of hot caramel into 8 coffee cups or 6 oz. ramekins, let cool until hard. Pour custard into cups, leave ½ inch from rim. Bake in a pre-heated 300° oven in a baking pan. Fill pan with water to midway of cups, cover with foil and poke 8 ½ inch holes in top. Bake until knife inserted comes out clean.

Françoise O'Neill

Freelance writer for Coastal Magazine, Better Homes & Gardens, Cottage Style and Sarasota resident.

Chai Spiced Crème Caramel with Raspberry

Serves 2

1 cup whole milk	3 whole cloves
1 cup heavy cream	1 cup granulated sugar
6 green or white cardamom pods	1 large egg
1 tsp. whole black peppercorns	1 large egg yolk
3 - 3 inch cinnamon sticks	1 tsp. fennel seeds
1/3 cup packed light brown sugar	1 cup fresh raspberries

- Preheat oven to 350°.
- Bring milk, cream, cardamom, peppercorns fennel seeds, cinnamon sticks and cloves to a boil in a heavy saucepan over medium heat. Remove from heat, cover and let stand 15 minutes.
- Cook sugar in a dry heavy saucepan over moderate heat, stirring constantly, until sugar melts and turns golden brown. Immediately pour caramelized sugar into 4-inch ramekins or small bowls, tilting to cover bottoms evenly.
- Whisk together whole egg and yolk in a large bowl. Bring spiced milk to a boil again. Add eggs in a slow stream, whisking constantly. Pour custard base through a fine sieve into a 2-cup measure. Add brown sugar and a pinch of salt stir until sugar is dissolved. Divide custard between the two ramekins.
- Bake custard in a water bath in middle of oven until set but still trembling slightly, about 30 minutes. Remove ramekins from water bath and cool crème caramels on a rack. Cover loosely and chill for at least 3 hours.
- Just before serving, run a knife around the inside edges of the ramekins. Arrange raspberries, open ends up over the entire surface on custards pressing gently to adhere.

The Ritz-Carlton Sarasota

1111 Ritz-Carlton Drive
Sarasota, FL 34236
941-309-2000

Citrus Crepe Layer Cake

Chef Stephane Cheramy

Delicious layers of crepes filled with an orange cream and caramel citrus sauce.

Serves 6

Crepe Batter
> 1 ¼ cup milk
> 3/4 cup cream
> 6 eggs
> 1/2 cup sugar
> 3/4 cup flour
> 1 vanilla bean, ground
> 1/8 cup Grand Marnier

✎ Mix all ingredients together. Refrigerate for one hour.

Pastry Cream
> 4 ¼ cups milk
> 4 egg yolks
> 1/2 cup flour
> 3/4 cup sugar
> 1/8 cup Grand Marnier
> 5 orange zests

🌿 Boil milk, mix egg yolks and sugar. Add flour and temper the mixture with a little bit of milk and cook together until boiling.

Caramel Sauce
1 cup sugar
1/2 cup water
1 cup orange juice

🌿 Heat sugar and water at low temperature; slowly add orange juice. Once combined allow to cool.

Cake assembly
🌿 Cook the crepes and build a cake on a cake mold with fine layers of cream between them. Refrigerate for 6 hours and remove the cake mold. Cut slices and serve with caramel sauce. Garnish with peeled orange segments.

Children at the Van Wezel

The Colony Resort

1620 Gulf of Mexico Drive
Longboat Key, FL 34238
941-383-5558

Chocolate Crepes with Cherry and Chocolate Crunch Filling

Chef Henry Martignago
Serves 8

1 lb. ripe Bing cherries
1 tsp. vanilla extract
2 tbsp. Kirsch
pinch of ground cinnamon
1 tbsp. lemon juice
1/4 cup granulated sugar
3 oz. bittersweet chocolate, cut into bits
vanilla ice cream or sweetened whipped cream
cocoa powder for dusting

Crepe Batter

2 tbsp. cocoa powder, preferable Dutch process
1/3 cup all purpose four
pinch of salt
2 tbsp. granulated sugar
2 eggs
3/4 cups milk, plus additional for thinning
1 tsp. vanilla extract
3 tbsp. unsalted butter, melted

Wash and pit the cherries. Place them in a bowl and run a knife through them to chop coarsely. Chop them in a bowl so as not to lose the juices.

Stir in the vanilla, kirsch, cinnamon, lemon juice and sugar, and let the cherries sit for 1 hour so they become a juicy filling.

To make the crepes, sift the cocoa, flour, salt and sugar into a mixing bowl. Make a well in the middle and add the eggs, milk, vanilla and melted butter. The batter should be the consistency of heavy cream: add more milk if necessary. Let the batter rest for at least 2 hours, (can hold in the refrigerator overnight).

Heat a seasoned crepe pan or a lightly buttered frying pan. The pan should be hot enough so that a drop of batter sizzles when tested. Add ladle of batter to the hot pan, quickly roll and turn the pan to spread the batter, then pour excess batter back in to the bowl. Cook until brown speckles appear on the other side.

When ready to serve, assemble the crepes. Stir chocolate bits into cherry filling. Place a large spoon of filling down the center of the crepe, and roll up the crepe. Place on individual plate. Continue to fill and roll crepes; serve 2 crepes to a plate.

Top each serving with a small scoop of vanilla ice cream or a large dollop of thick whipped cream. Place a small amount of cocoa in a sieve and quickly dust the top of each serving.

Circle Sculpture at Selby Gardens

175

Javier's Restaurant and Wine Bar

1620 Gulf of Mexico Drive
Longboat Key, FL 34238
941-383-5558

Chocolate Decadence Torte

Imagine a cross between melt-in-your-mouth chocolate fudge and a chewy walnut brownie, covered with a chocolate rum ganache, served with a large scoop of vanilla ice cream.

Serves 8

> 1/2 cup butter
> 3 eggs
> 2/3 cup light corn syrup
> 1 tsp. vanilla
> 1 1/4   cup chopped semi-sweet chocolate
> 1 cup flour
> 1/2 cup sugar
> 1 cup chopped walnuts

🍃 Generously butter and flour a 9-inch round cake pan.

🍃 Melt butter and corn syrup together. Add chocolate and stir until melted and well blended. Mix in sugar until well blended. Beat in eggs and vanilla. Stir in four and walnuts.

🍃 Pour into pan and bake at 350° for about 25 minutes. **Do not over bake** – the torte is done when the center is slightly rounded and just barely springs back when touched.

🍃 Let cool in pan about 10 minutes then turn into rack and let cool completely.

Ganache:

    2 tbsp. butter
    1 tbsp. light corn syrup
    1 cup chopped semi-sweet chocolate
    2 tbsp. spiced rum

Melt together the butter and corn syrup. Stir in the chocolate until smooth, well blended and shiny. Stir in the rum. Pour over the torte then spread with a spatula to drip down the sides. Chill. The torte is easier to slice if cut before completely chilled. Serve with vanilla ice cream and whipped cream.

Washingtonian Palms on Bayfront

Cru Bistro and Wine Bar

1377 Main Street
Sarasota, FL 34236
941-951-NAPA

Bruciata Italiana (Crème Brulee)

Chef Chris Covelli

Serves 4

Note: Have on hand 4 – 4 oz. ramekins. Also note when infusing other flavors the flavor should be steeped in the heavy cream mixture.

> 4 egg yolks
> 6 tbsp. sugar
> 2 ½ cups heavy cream
> ½ vanilla bean or 2 Tbsp. vanilla extract
> very small pinch of salt

- Put heavy cream, vanilla bean or vanilla extract in a saucepan and bring to a rolling boil. Take off the stove and place in ice bath to cool.
- While heavy cream mixture cools, whisk together egg yolks, a pinch of salt and sugar until you reach a pale yellow color and double in volume.
- When the heavy cream mixture is cool, add 1/3 of it to the egg yolk/sugar mixture until well combined. After you have tempered the mixture add the rest of the heavy cream mixture until well combined.
- Place the ramekins in a sheet cake pan and add enough water until water level is half way up the sides of the ramekins.
- Cook at 300° for 50 minutes or until custard is set. Remove from the oven and let cool.
- Sprinkle some fine white sugar on top of each custard and caramelize with a torch or under broiler just before serving.

Fleming's Steakhouse and Wine Bar

2001 Siesta Drive
Sarasota, FL 34232
941-358-9463

Fleming's Chocolate Lava Cake

Chef Russell Skall

Serves 6

> 3/4 lb butter, lightly salted
> 3/4 lb. semisweet chocolate
> 5 whole eggs
> 3 egg yolks
> 3/4 cup sugar
> 2+ tbsp. flour

- Cut butter and chocolate into small pieces then place in a mixing bowl set over top of a double boiler with simmering water. Heat the butter and chocolate until melted.

- While chocolate is melting combine whole eggs and egg yolks in a mixing bowl and whip until slightly thick. Add sugar to eggs and whip for 1 minute to blend.

- Lightly whip the chocolate and the butter until smooth. Add the egg mixture to the chocolate and mix well. Fold in flour and combine well into chocolate mixture. Spread additional room temperature butter and flour in 6 small cups. Combine butter and flour making a smooth paste. Make sure to cover all areas in the cup. Fill each cup equally with batter to about half an inch from the top. Cook cake in 350° oven for 18 – 20 minutes until it is firm on top with a slight crust.

- Remove the cake from the oven and allow to cool for 1 – 2 minutes. Carefully tip cup onto a plate. Garnish with raspberry sauce or chocolate sauce and fresh berries.

Roy's Hawaiian Fusion

2000 Siesta Drive
Sarasota, FL 34239
941-952-0109

Roy's Chocolate Soufflé

Chef Roy Yamaguchi

Serves 4
Note: recipe must cool overnight.

6 tbsp. unsalted butter	1 3/4 tbsp cornstarch
4 oz. semi sweet chocolate	2 eggs plus 2 egg yolks
3/4 cup sugar	

- In a saucepan over low heat, melt the butter and chocolate together. Set aside.
- In a mixing bowl, combine the sugar and cornstarch. In a separate bowl; whisk the eggs and yolks together. Add the melted bitter chocolate mixture to the sugar mixture and combine thoroughly with a wire whisk. Stir in the eggs and whisk just until smooth. Place in the refrigerator overnight.
- Remove from refrigerator and strain into a clean container. Cover with plastic wrap. Press down to prevent a skim from forming. Refrigerate again for 3 to 4 hours. Must be well chilled.
- Preheat oven to 400°. Line 4 metal rings, about 2 ¾" across and 2" deep with greased parchment paper. Line a baking sheet with parchment paper and set the molds on the sheet. Scoop the mixture into the molds so they are two thirds full. Make sure the molds are not leaking.
- Bake on the top rack of oven for 20 minutes. Remove the baking sheet from the oven and while holding each mold with tongs, slide a metal spatula underneath, carefully lift and transfer to a serving plate. Gently lift off the mold and remove the parchment paper. Serve immediately.
- Feel free to add a fresh raspberry sauce or sprinkle with powdered sugar. 180

Dessert Bete Noir

Serves 12

18 oz. dark chocolate
1 lb. butter
¾ cup water
2 cups granulated sugar
8 eggs

- Chop chocolate and butter and place in a bowl.
- Bring 1 ½ cups sugar to a boil with ¾ cup water. Pour this mixture over chocolate and butter and stir until mixed and melted.
- Preheat oven to 375°.
- Mix eggs with remaining ½ cup of sugar until ribbon stage.
- Fold eggs into chocolate. Pour mixture into parchment lined and greased 9" x 12" pan. Bake in water bath for 45 minutes to 1 hour until set. Cool in refrigerator over night.
- To serve flip out onto cutting board and cut into small serving pieces. Puddle raspberry sauce on plate, place chocolate on top of sauce and dot with whipped cream if desired.

Raspberry Sauce

2 pints raspberries
1 cup sugar
½ cup water

- Place raspberries, sugar and water in saucepan. Bring to a boil, reduce by half.
- Strain through fine sieve and cool.

Caragiulo's Italian Restaurant

69 South Palm Avenue
Downtown Sarasota, FL 34236
(941) 951-0866

Chocolate Espresso Torte

Henry Ohlanf
Serves 8 to 10

1/2 lb. bittersweet Belgian chocolate
1/2 lb. sugar   2 oz. strong espresso (brewed)
1/2 lb. butter   1 oz. Kahlua
3 whole eggs   1/2 tsp. vanilla extract
3 egg yolks

🖎 In a double boiler — combine, sugar, chocolate and butter. Stir until sugar dissolves and chocolate melts (approx. ½ hour).

🖎 In a separate bowl, beat eggs lightly.

🖎 Remove chocolate mix from heat, add espresso, Kahlua and vanilla and stir well.

🖎 Slowly add chocolate mix to eggs, mixing slowly to temper the eggs. Mix well to a smooth consistency.

🖎 Butter a small cake pan and line the insides with parchment paper. Add the chocolate mix.

🖎 Cook in a water bath at 350° for about 1 hour or until a toothpick inserted comes out clean.

🖎 Cool to room temperature and refrigerate overnight.

🖎 Cut into portions and serve with fresh whipped cream and sliced fresh berries.

Simply Gourmet

4783 Swift Road
Sarasota, FL 34233
941-929-0066

Chocolate Fondue Grand Mariner

Chef Larry Barrett

> 2 cups heavy cream
> 12 oz. chopped semi-sweet chocolate
> 1 tbsp. unsalted butter (room temperature)
> 2 tbsp. Grand Mariner

Heat cream on stovetop until it steams; remove from heat. Add chocolate all at once. Stir slowly until chocolate melts and becomes satiny smooth, this may take a few minutes.

Add the butter and stir until it melts and is incorporated. Add the Grand Mariner and stir. Serve with sliced fruit and pound cake wedges.

This chocolate fondue is a simple dessert, but what a delicious indulgence. Use a fine European style chocolate; it makes all the difference. I serve the fondue with fresh fruit like strawberries, pineapple and a pound cake medley. You can even roll the chocolate covered fruit and pound cake in chopped toasted nuts — shame on me! Do not present the fondue in a standard fondue pot with a flame. The heat will separate the cocoa solids and cocoa utter. Put the melted fondue in small warmed ramekins, one for every two guests.

Caragiulo's Italian Restaurant

69 South Palm Avenue
Downtown Sarasota, FL 34236
(941) 951-0866

Chocolate Cheesecake

Serves 10

> 2 lbs. softened cream cheese
> 3/4 cup milk
> 1 ½ cup sugar
> 4 eggs
> 1 tsp. vanilla
> 1 pint sour cream
> 1/2 cup flour
> 1/2 cup powdered cocoa

🌿 Put all ingredients in a mixing bowl, one item at a time. Blend until creamy.

🌿 Pour into a greased and floured 10-inch spring form pan.

🌿 Bake at 325° for 1 hour, and then turn off oven. Leave oven door open and allow to settle. Refrigerate 3 to 4 hours before serving.

Piecrust is optional with this recipe.

J Ryan on the Grill

8389 South Tamiami Trail
Sarasota, FL 34231
941-923-3200

J Ryan's Key Lime Cheesecake

Chef Christian Bousquet

Serves 10

1 ¾ cups graham cracker crumbs
1 tsp. vanilla
5 tbsp. butter, melted
3 eggs
½ cup fresh limejuice
1 cup plus 1 tbsp. sugar
3– 8 oz. packages cream cheese, softened
whipped cream

🍃 Pre-heat oven to 350°. Make the crust by combining graham cracker crumbs with the butter and 1 tbsp. sugar in a medium bowl. Stir to coat all the crumbs with butter, keeping it crumbly. Press crumbs onto the bottom and about half way up the sides of an 8-inch spring form pan. Bake the crust for 5 minutes, then set-aside until ready to fill.

🍃 In a large mixing bowl, combine cream cheese, 1 cup sugar and vanilla. Mix with an electric beater until smooth. Add the lime juice and eggs and continue to beat until smooth and creamy.

🍃 Pour filling into the pan. Bake for 60-70 minutes until the top of the cheesecake turns light brown. Remove from oven and allow to cool.

🍃 When cheesecake is room temperature, put into the refrigerator to chill. Serve with a dollop of whipped cream and some grated lime zest.

Turtle's Restaurant

8875 Midnight Pass Road
Siesta Key, FL 34242
(941) 346-2207

Irish Coffee Cheesecake

Chef Eric Brown
Serves 8

> 6 whole eggs
> 3 lb. cream cheese
> 1 lb. brown sugar
> 3 cups coffee – reduced to ½ cup
> 1/3 cup Kahlua
> 2 tbsp. vanilla
> 1/4 cup Irish whiskey
> 8 oz. Oreo cookies

🍃 Cream eggs, brown sugar, reduced coffee, Kahlua, vanilla, and Irish whiskey until smooth. Add cream cheese and blend until smooth.

Crust

🍃 Line the bottom of a spring form pan evenly with 8 oz. of Oreo cookie crumbs that have been finely ground.

🍃 Pack crumbs down tightly. Pour in cheesecake mixture.

🍃 Bake at 300° for 1 hour and 15 minutes. Pull out of oven and allow to cool to room temperature. Chill for 3 to 4 hours before serving.

Roessler's Restaurant

2033 Vamo Way
South Sarasota, FL 34229
941-966-5688

Goat Cheese Cheesecake

Klaus Roessler

16 oz. Goat cheese
8 oz. cream cheese

🍃 Bring to room temperature. Mix together.

Add

1 cup heavy cream
4 whipped eggs
1 ½ cups white sugar

🍃 Pour mixture into ceramic cups that have been wiped inside with butter and then sugar.

🍃 Bake in a water bath at 350° for 45 minutes or until a metal knife inserted in the middle comes out clean.

Cherry Sauce

🍃 Bring juice of canned Bing cherries to a boil. Add port wine and reduce on medium heat until syrupy. Add a touch of cornstarch to thicken if necessary.

🍃 Add cherries.

🍃 Serve sauce chilled over top of cheesecake.

Jan & Judi's Favorite Recipes

Adonidia Palm (also known as Christmas Palm)

Good Friends and Good Food
What could be better?

Stuffed French Toast

Serves 6

Whether it is a fabulous Sunday Brunch or a hot summer's night dinner, this recipe blends the richness of Challah bread and marscapone cheese with fresh berries for an all time favorite.

> 1 loaf Challah bread, sliced thick
> 1 lb. cream cheese
> 1/2 cup marscapone cheese
> 3 tbsp. powdered sugar
> 1 tsp. vanilla extract
> 2 tbsp. Grand Marnier liquor
> 3 eggs, beaten with milk
> 1 tbsp. cinnamon
> 1 fresh peach, cored and sliced
> 1/2 cup fresh blueberries
> 1/2 cup fresh strawberries or raspberries
> 1/4 cup brown sugar
> dash of Chambord liquor (optional)

🍃 Whip softened cream cheese, marscapone, Grand Marnier, vanilla and powdered sugar until fluffy. Spread cream cheese mixture on six slices of bread, top with another slice of bread and set aside.

🍃 In saucepan add butter to coat pan, add peach slices, strawberries, blueberries and brown sugar. Add a dash of Chambord to taste.

🍃 In medium hot griddle, brown bread on both sides.

🍃 To serve, cut bread in half and place on plate. Top with warm fruit and serve immediately.

Judi Gallagher's
Cream of Pumpkin Soup

Memories of New England- This recipe found its way on to my daily specials board of "Main Street Café" north of Boston on many a chilly day.

2 tbsp. butter
1/2 onion, thinly sliced
1/2 tbsp. flour
10 oz. chicken broth
1 can pumpkin (1 lb.)
2 cups milk
1 cup light cream
1 tsp. salt
1/8 tsp. pepper
1/4 tsp. ginger
1/8 tsp. cinnamon
crème fraishe to garnish

- In a hot 6-quart pot, melt butter. Sauté onion, stirring occasionally until tender. Remove from heat.
- Stir in flour gradually add chicken broth. Bring to a boil, reduce heat and simmer covered for 10 minutes.
- Ladle mixture unto blender and blend until completely smooth.
- Return to pot and whisk in pumpkin. Add milk, cream and 2 cups water and the seasonings. Whip with wire whisk until blended.
- Heat soup until just before boiling point. Serve in hollowed out small pumpkins. Top with crème fraiche and dried cranberries and diced Macintosh apples.

For more cooking tips make sure you turn your radio to 1220 WIBQ every Tuesday and Thursday from 1-2 p.m., or log on to www.Newstalk1220.com and click on the live button for "Cooking in Paradise".

Pat McCann's

Spinach and Bleu Cheese Salad

Serves 6

This recipe originally from Vegetarian Times magazine brings plenty of nutrients and a bit of spring into your daily routine.

Salad

      1/4 cup sunflower seeds, roasted
      1 – 6 oz. bag baby spinach
      1 large apple, sliced
      1/2 cup crumbled blue cheese

🌱 Place sunflower seeds in medium sized skillet. Toast over medium heat 5 to 6 minutes or until browned and fragrant. Shake pan often. Transfer to a small bowl and cool.

🌱 Just before serving, toss spinach, sliced apple, crumbled cheese and cooled sunflower seeds with vinaigrette. Divide salad among 6 salad plates.

Cider Vinaigrette

      2 tbsp. cider vinegar
      1 tbsp. Dijon mustard
      1 tbsp. honey
      1/2 tsp. salt
      1/4 tsp. black pepper
      3 tbsp. olive oil
      2 tbsp. water
      1 shallot, minced

🌱 Combine vinegar, mustard, honey, salt and pepper in a small bowl. Whisk in oil and water. Stir in shallots.

Jan McCann's friend Monique Fisher's

Goat Cheese Salad

🍃 Mix several kinds of lettuce in a bowl with vinaigrette dressing (recipe follows). Add sliced green pepper, garbanzo beans, olives (black and green), sliced onion and sliced cucumber.

🍃 Toast white bread and cut into squares. Put one slice of goat cheese on each square and put under broiler for about 1 minute — until warm but not melted. Arrange on top of salad bowl and serve.

Viniagrette:
    3 tbsp. olive oil
    1 tbsp. red wine vinegar
    1 tbsp. Dijon mustard
    1 large clove of garlic salt and pepper

🍃 Mix together and pour over salad. This is authentic French vinaigrette.

Marina Jack's

Linda Thomas's

Beet Salad

Photographer and good friend
Sarasota Resident

This recipe is my "Big Gramma's" She lived on a farm with pigs and chickens. She grew her own vegetables, beets of course. I remember her, dipping chickens in boiling water and plucking them, which then became dinner.

3 bunches baby beets
1/3 cup extra virgin olive oil
Kosher salt and fresh ground pepper
1 tsp. balsamic vinegar
4 oz. gorgonzola cheese
1 handful toasted walnut halves
1/2 cup celery leaves

Bring water to a boil, add beets. Cook until the beets are knife tender, about 30 to 40 minutes. Rub off the tuff outer beet skins under cold running water with a soft cloth.

Slice and toss the beets with extra virgin olive oil, balsamic vinegar, salt and pepper and toasted walnut halves. Sprinkle with gorgonzola cheese and garnish with celery leaves.

I added gorgonzola to Gramma's recipe for extra flavor! She would not mind.

Jan McCann's
New Potato Salad

I like this potato salad because there is no mayonnaise.

Makes 4 to 6 servings

2 lbs. sweet potatoes, peeled and cut into 1 inch cubes
vegetable cooking spray
3/4 tsp. salt divided
2 celery ribs, diced
1 jalapeno pepper, seeded finely chopped
1/2 cup diced onion
1/3 cup diced green bell pepper
3 tbsp. brown sugar
2 tbsp. chopped fresh or 1 Tbsp. dried parsley flakes
5 tbsp. white vinegar
1 tbsp. vegetable oil
1 tsp. hot sauce
3 slices peppered or regular bacon, cooked and crumbled

Garnish fresh flat leaf parsley sprigs.

Arrange potatoes in an even layer in a 15 x 10" jelly roll pan. Coat with cooking spray, and sprinkle with 1/2 tsp. salt.

Bake at 400° for 25 minutes or just until tender. Let cool slightly.

Stir together remaining 1/4 tsp salt, celery and next 9 ingredients in a large bowl until blended. Add potatoes, and toss gently to coat. Sprinkle with crumbled bacon, if desired, garnish, if desired. Serve warm or chilled.

German Potato Salad

This is the real deal!!

    5 medium potatoes, cooked and sliced
    6 slices bacon, cooked & crumbled
    1 medium onion chopped

Sauce:

    1-3/4 tbsp. flour
    bacon drippings
    ½ cup water
    ½ cup sugar
    ½ cup vinegar
    salt and pepper to taste

Stir flour into bacon drippings. Add sugar, vinegar, and water. Boil until thick.

Alternate layers of potatoes, onions, bacon, salt and pepper. Pour sauce over all.

Serve immediately, or cover and re-heat in slow oven about 30 minutes. Best when made a day ahead and reheated.

Great for picnics. I usually double the recipe.

Frank Creaturo's (my favorite local artist)

Fried Eggplant

Creaturo Gallery
1269 First Street
Sarasota, FL 34236
941-953-6163

Makes a great appetizer or light supper.

> 3 eggplants, peeled and sliced thin
> 1/2 cup olive oil
> 3 tbsp. soy sauce
> 2 tsp. Dijon mustard
> handful fresh basil
> 2 garlic cloves, chopped
> 1/4 cup grated Parmesan cheese

🌿 Lightly coat pan with Pam or cooking oil. Fry the eggplant on both sides.

🌿 Lay eggplant out on tray to cool.

🌿 Line tray with lettuce leaves and place cooled eggplant on top. Slice some tomatoes and place one tomato slice in the center of each eggplant.

🌿 Put remaining ingredients in blender and blend. Pour the mixture over the eggplant a half hour before serving to allow flavors to marry. To finish sprinkle with logattelli slivers or Parmesano Reggiano cheese and season with salt.

"Eat vegetables and fear no creditors,
rather than eat duck and hide."

—Hebrew Proverb

Judi Gallagher's

Zucchini Cheese Flan

Serves 6 to 8

This is a favorite recipe that Marimar Torres shared with me last summer during a visit to her winery. It has become such a hit that friends have all borrowed the recipe and makes it on a regular basis now. Served with Margrit Mondavi's vinaigrette, tossed into field greens and chopped romaine, this is a perfect summer meal or salad and vegetable course for your next dinner party.

> 3/4 tsp. salt
> 3 lbs. (about 10 medium) zucchini, grated
> 3 tbsp. butter
> 1 large onion, minced
> 1 cup ricotta cheese
> 3 cups grated Monterey Jack cheese
> 3 eggs beaten
> fresh ground pepper to taste

- Sprinkle 3/4 tsp. salt over grated zucchini and let sit for 15 minutes to release liquid. Squeeze inside a cloth and discard liquid.

- Preheat oven to 375°. Heat 1 tbsp. butter in a medium skillet and sauté onion slowly for about 10 minutes. Transfer to bowl. Add remaining 2 tbsp. butter to skillet and sauté zucchini for 10 minutes. Transfer to bowl and let cool.

- Add ricotta cheese, 2 ½ cups grated cheese, eggs, remaining salt and black pepper. Mix well and adjust seasoning if needed.

- Oil or butter muffin pans and pour mixture into pans. Top with remaining grated cheese. Bake at 375° until cheese on top is brown. Let cool about 20 minutes. Remove from muffin pans. Serve with field greens and chopped romaine lettuce tossed with your favorite vinaigrette.

Judi Gallagher's
Sautéed Scallops Key West

Serves 4

> 1 lb. sea scallops, patted dry
> all purpose flour
> 1 tbsp. olive oil
> 2 tbsp. plus 1 tbsp. butter
> 1 shallot, minced
> 2 tbsp. fresh lemon juice
> 2 tbsp. fresh lime juice
> 2 tbsp. gold tequila
> 1 tbsp. triple sec
>
> 1 tbsp. lemon zest
> 1 tbsp. lime zest

✎ Sprinkle scallops with salt and pepper to taste. Dust with flour. Heat oil in large skillet over high heat.

✎ Add scallops to hot pan. Sauté until brown and just cooked through, about 2-3 minutes per side. Remove from heat using tongs. Transfer scallops to platter.

✎ Add butter and shallots to skillet and sauté until golden. Add lemon juice, limejuice. Reduce for 30 seconds. Remove pan from heat to avoid a flame and add tequila and triple sec.

✎ Place pan on burner, reduce slightly. Add 1 tbsp. of butter to sauce to make a smooth finish. Pour over scallops. Top with citrus zest.

✎ Place pan over medium-low heat. Season sauce with salt and pepper. Spoon over scallops. Sprinkle a little more zest over scallops before serving.

Judi Gallagher's

Panko Crusted Salmon with Vegetable Tempura

Serves 2

When purchasing salmon, I prefer to buy with skin on which helps to hold the fish together while cooking. The skin also adds a nice crispness but many people do not like the skin, either way is fine but please note that fried fish skin is quite a delicacy and pulls off easily after cooking.

> 2 - 7 ounce fillets of salmon
> 2 cups Panko crumbs (Japanese bread crumbs)
> 1 tbsp. freshly grated ginger
> 1 tbsp. freshly diced lemon grass or a squeeze from the tube
>   lemongrass (can be found in the produce section of store)
> kosher salt and fresh ground white pepper
> canola or peanut oil

- Coat bottom of fry pan with oil.

- Heat pan on medium high heat. Rub salmon fillet with grated ginger and lemongrass. Press into panko crumbs on both sides. Season with salt and pepper to taste.

- Drop salmon in hot oil and sear on both sides. Approximately 3 minutes on each side for medium rare. Serve with Tempura vegetables.

Tempura batter is quite easy and can be used directly on fish and chicken tenderloins as well as fresh vegetables. Batter recipe is on the next page.

Tempura Batter:

    12 ounces all purpose flour
    Ice cold club soda or sparkling water
    1 egg
    3 lbs. of assorted vegetables (see below)

✎ Place flour in large mixing bowl. With the handle of a long spoon, mix and stir in ice-cold soda or water. Stir until the mixture is slightly thicker than the consistency of buttermilk. Make a point of not over mixing. Tempura batter should be lumpy and is renowned for lumps of flour.

✎ Any vegetables will work but these are the most commonly used, zucchini, red onions, eggplants, sweet potatoes, string beans, broccoli, wild mushrooms, asparagus, button mushrooms and bok choy. Any vegetables will work but these are the most commonly used. Dip sliced vegetables, into batter mixture and shake off excess.

✎ Deep fry vegetables in a wok or deep fat fryer. You can use a frying pan if you do not have a wok or deep fryer. Fill pan with 3 inches of clean peanut or canola oil. Heat oil to 400 degrees. Fry vegetables until light golden in color. Turn the vegetables at intervals to ensure that both sides are cooked equally. Remove vegetables from oil with slotted spoon and place on paper towels. Serve immediately.

Tempura dipping sauce:

    1 cup rice wine vinegar
    2 tbsp. sugar
    1/2 handful cilantro, chopped
    1 small chili pepper, seeded finely chopped
    1/2 tsp. chopped garlic
    salt and pepper

✎ Pour rice wine vinegar into a small bowl. Add sugar and stir until sugar dissolved. Taste for sweetness. Add cilantro, chili and garlic mix well. Season with salt and pepper and allow to sit for 10 minutes to 1 hour for flavors to combine.

Judi Gallagher's

Grilled Shrimp with Apricot, Mango & Chipolte Glaze on Chopped Asian Salad

Serves 4

You will need Kozlowski Farms Apricot, Mango Chipotle sauce for this recipe. You can get this at Southgate Gourmet or on line at www.KozlowskiFarms.com

> 12 large shrimp, peeled and deveined
> bamboo skewers, soaked in water for thirty minutes.
> 1/2 cup chopped macadamia nuts (optional)
> 1 head Romaine lettuce, chopped
> 1/2 head Napa cabbage, chopped
> 1 red pepper, diced
> 1 small can mandarin oranges, drained
> 1 cup fresh bean sprouts
> 1/2 cup snow peas, julienne

✎ Chop vegetables and toss in a chilled bowl. Toss with dressing just before serving.

> 1 package bean thread noodles

✎ Drop bean threads in pot of hot canola oil for about 3-5 second. The bean threads will immediately turn white and puff to fullness. Remove and place on paper towel.

Asian Dressing

    1 tsp. fresh grated ginger
    1/2 cup low sodium soy sauce
    2 cups rice wine vinegar
    1/4 cup sesame oil
    1 tsp. fresh garlic
    1/2 tsp. Szechwan fire sauce (optional)

  Blend ginger, garlic, sesame oil, rice wine vinegar and soy sauce together. If you want this dressing spicier, add Szechwan fire sauce.

  Skewer shrimp and brush with Apricot Chipotle sauce. Grill appox. 3 minutes until pink and tender. Brush with more apricot glaze.

For Assembly:

Arrange salad in the center of chilled plate. Top with white bean thread noodles. Arrange one or two skewers with shrimp coming out of the center of the salad. Garnish with a sprinkle of chopped macadamia nuts and a crisp wonton if desired.

Recipe works well with lemon grass seared scallops as well as hoi sin glazed salmon. Make a large portion of the Asian Vinaigrette and keep covered in the refrigerator for many simple pan seared seafood recipes.

Jan McCann's famous
London Broil
Handed down from my parents

Marinate London broil overnight or for 2 days, the longer the better.

🍃 Use half a bottle of red wine that you like to drink.

🍃 Mix the wine with ½ cup brown sugar.

🍃 Add healthy splash of Worcestershire sauce and soy sauce.

🍃 Sprinkle with garlic powder or crush several cloves of garlic in with the wine mixture.

🍃 Immerse London broil also called flank steak into the marinade.

🍃 Grill over a hot fire until charred on the outside and serve rare.

I usually cook about 11 minutes on the first side and 8 minutes on second side depending on thickness of meat. Cut across the grain into thin strips. Serve with potatoes and red wine.

Pat McCann's
Oven Baked Ribs

A family favorite and so easy to make!

Country style ribs work best. Buy as many as you want.

- Bake ribs in 325° oven for at least an hour. Pour off fat.

- Slice whole onion very thin and cover the ribs with the onion slices. Pour your favorite bar-b-que sauce over the onions to cover completely.

- Cover the pan with tin foil.

- Bake for an additional 2 1/2 hours.

You might want to throw a couple of potatoes in the oven during the last hour the ribs are cooking for a complete meal.

The key to a long life:
Live honestly,
Eat slowly and
Lie about your age!
Lucille Ball

Jan McCann's
Instant Duck Breast

Fast and easy for a week night dinner.

Serves 2

Buy frozen boneless duck breasts. Set out to thaw.

> 2 tbsp. butter
> 2 tbsp Worcestershire sauce
> 1 cup beef stock
> 3 tbsp. blackberry jam - highest quality available
> 1 cup milk
> 2 tbsp. cornstarch
> 1 tbsp. cream sherry

🍃 Melt butter in small saucepan. Add beef base, jam and Worcestershire sauce and combine. Add water and milk and stir over medium heat. When almost to a boil combine cornstarch with a tbsp. of water and add to sauce stirring constantly. Remove from heat when thickened.

🍃 Heat skillet on high heat. Sear duck breasts skin side down first. Cook 8 minutes turn and cook 8 minutes on second side. Remove from heat and let duck rest for 10 minutes. Serve with sauce.

The first ever cookbook in the United States was published in 1824.

Gene's Marinated Chuck Roast

My Dad (Gene) would makes this on a routine basis growing up. We lived in Michigan so he would scrape the snow off the Weber before firing up the grill many a week night.

Makes one 3-4 lb. roast

> 1 chuck roast, 1 ½" thick
> 1/4 cup olive oil
> 1/3 cup soy sauce
> 2 cloves garlic, smashed
> 3 tbsp. red wine vinegar
> 1/4 cup brown sugar
> 1/4 cup bourbon
> 1 ¼ cups beef broth or water

Pour marinade over roast and refrigerate overnight.

When grill is ready and gray coals are spread, drain roast and broil 30 – 40 minutes, longer on the second side as fire diminishes. Please turn only once to keep juices in.

Judi Gallagher's

Stuffed Flank Steak with Port Wine Reduction

Serves 3 - 4

3 lb flank steak
garlic salt
fresh ground pepper
1 red pepper cut into strips
1 yellow pepper cut into strips
1 sliced onion
olive oil
1/2 lb. fresh sautéed baby Portobello mushrooms

4 - 6 slices imported Prosciutto
4 slices smoked provolone
4 - 6 sun-dried tomatoes
1/2 cup demi glace
1/2 cup port wine
fresh arugula

- Sprinkle flank steak with garlic salt and fresh ground pepper. In hot sauté pan with 1 Tbsp. olive oil, sauté peppers and onions. Add sautéed mushrooms.
- Spread out seasoned flank steak. Layer Prosciutto and provolone. On top of Prosciutto and provolone, add sautéed vegetables, spread to the edges. Place sun dried tomatoes on top. Roll the flank steak in jellyroll fashion. Add 1-2 tbsp. olive oil to very hot fry pan. Sear meat, turning often. Remove when browned on all sides. Place in preheated 400° oven for about 10 minutes for medium rare.
- In the same pan that you browned the flank steak in, deglaze by adding demi-glace and port wine. Simmer and reduce by half using a wire whisk constantly.
- To serve: slice meat 3/4" thick. On a dinner plate, pour a small puddle of port wine sauce. Lay one slice of stuffed flank steak over the edge of the other. Top with more sauce. Roll fresh arugula and tuck gently into the sliced steak. Serve with rosemary roasted red potatoes.

Cooking time approximately 45 minutes including prep time.
Suggested wine Gamay Beaujolais

Judi Gallagher's

Roast Pork Tenderloin with Fennel, Parmesan and Dijon Crust
Serves 4 - 6

This can be roasted in the oven in a traditional pan with fingerling potatoes and sliced carrots, turnips and onions or on a soaked maple wood plank for added flavor.

1/2 cup beer (optional) ¼ cup olive oil
1/2 cup Dijon mustard   2 tbsp. fennel seeds
2 tbsp. chopped garlic   2 tbsp. Worcestershire sauce
2 lb. boneless pork loin roast
6 tbsp. freshly grated Parmesan cheese
garlic salt and fresh ground pepper to taste

1/4 cup light cream
1 tsp. gravy master
roux

✎ Whisk all ingredients aside from the pork to blend in 8x8x2 " glass baking dish. Add pork and turn to coat. Let stand at room temp. 1 hour or cover and refrigerate overnight, turning occasionally.

✎ Preheat oven to 350°. Transfer pork to rack set in roasting pan, reserve marinade. Season roast and top with a sprinkles of freshly grated Parmesan cheese. Roast until thermometer inserted into center registers 150°, about 55 minutes. Let stand 15 minutes.

✎ Strain marinade into heavy medium saucepan. Add juices from roasting pan. Boil sauce until reduced by half. Thicken with a roux, (equal parts of flour and melted butter), stirring constantly for about 15 minutes. Season with salt and pepper. Add 1 teaspoon of gravy master if desired and ¼ cup light cream. Stir until thick and reduced slightly.

✎ Slice pork and arrange on platter. Drizzle some sauce over. Serve, passing extra sauce separately. Serve roast with vegetables from pan or Wasabi mashed potatoes.

Judi Gallagher's
Baked Lemon Pudding

Serves 6

The top is cake like. The soft lemon custard beneath provides the sauce. For a richer dessert, spread the chilled pudding with a thin layer of unsweetened whipped cream.

> 1 cup sugar
> 1/2 cup flour
> 1/2 tsp. baking powder
> 1/4 tsp. salt
> 3 eggs separated
> 1/2 cup sugar
> 2 tsp. grated lemon rind
> 1/4 cup lemon juice
> 2 tbsp. melted butter
> 1 ½ cups milk
>
> 1 tbsp. lemon curd, chilled
> Fresh whipped cream
> Mint sprigs

🍃 Preheat oven to 350°. Butter a 2 quart baking dish.

🍃 Sift together sugar, flour, and baking powder, salt. Separate eggs. Beat the egg whites until stiff. Add sugar a spoonful at a time to the egg whites. Set aside. Without washing the beater, beat the yolks until light. Add grated lemon rind. Lemon juice, melted butter, milk. Stir into the flour mixture. Beat until smooth. Add the beaten whites and fold gently until no white flecks show. Pour into the baking dish.

🍃 Set in a pan of hot water 1/2 inch deep. Bake 45 minutes. Chill for half and hour. Top with a dollop of lemon curd and fresh whipped cream and mint sprigs.

Judi Gallagher's

The Original Main Street Café's Carrot Cake with Cream Cheese Frosting

The memories of carrot cakes baking and filling my first little breakfast and lunch café still bring a smile to my face. Of course, grating those many carrots often was not as pleasing as the final results. Today, with food processors and grocery stores that sell shredded carrots you really can have your cake and eat it too!

> 1 1/2 cup sugar
> 1 cup vegetable oil
> 3 large eggs
> 4 oz. cream cheese
> 2 cups all purpose flour
> 1 1/2 tsp. cinnamon
> 1 tsp. baking soda
> 1 tsp. vanilla
> 1/2 tsp. nutmeg (optional)
> 3 cups shredded carrots
> 1 cup coarsely chopped nuts, pecans
> 1 cup raisins

- Pre-heat oven to 350°. Grease a 9 x 13 pan and lightly dust with flour.
- Cream sugar with vegetable oil. Add softened cream cheese and eggs, one at a time.
- Sift flour with dry ingredients and gently beat into egg and sugar mixture.
- Add raisins, pecans, shredded carrots. Pour into pan.
- Bake approximately 40 – 45 minutes.

Frosting:

    8 oz. cream cheese, softened
    1/4 cup butter, softened
    2 tsp. milk
    1 tsp. pure vanilla extract
    4 cups powdered sugar

Whip soft cream cheese with butter. Add milk and vanilla extract. Slowly blend in powdered sugar. Frost cake, when cake is completely cooled. Refregerate for at least 3 hours before serving. Serve cold.

Entrance to New College

Pat McCann family favorite

Apple Dumplings

3 cups water
2 ¼ cups sugar
1/2 tsp. ground cinnamon
1/2 tsp. ground nutmeg
12 drops red food coloring
¼ cup butter
2 ½ cups sifted all-purpose flour
½ tsp sugar
1/3 cup cold skim milk
½ cup + 1 tbsp. canola oil
6 small whole apples pared and cored.

For the syrup
Mix first 5 ingredients cook 5 minutes. Remove from heat: add butter.

For pie crust:
Mix flour and sugar in bowl. Pour milk and oil into the same measuring cup. Do not stir. Add all at once to the flour. Stir with a fork until well-blended and them form into a smooth ball with hands. Roll out using short brisk strokes, between two 18 x 12 inch squares of waxed paper until dough is ½ " thick and or reaches edge of paper. Cut into six, 6" squares.

Assembly:
Place an apple on each square of pastry. Sprinkle apples generously with additional sugar, cinnamon and nutmeg and dot with butter. Moisten edges of pastry. Bring corners to center and pinch together. Place one inch apart in ungreased 13" x 9" x 2" baking pan. Pour syrup over the dumplings. Bake at 375 F for 35 – 40 minutes. Serve warm with cream or vanilla ice cream.

Date Cake

This recipe has been handed down through several generations.

Pre-heat oven to 350°.

> 1 cup chopped dates
> 1 tsp. soda, sprinkled over dates

Pour: 1 cup boiling water over dates and soda and let cool

Mix: 1 cup sugar

           scant 1/3 cup shortening

           1 egg, beaten

Add: 1 ½ cups sifted flour

           1 tsp. vanilla

           1/2 tsp. salt

Add: date mixture

While cake bakes, mix:

           5 tbsp. brown sugar

           3 tbsp. melted butter

           3 tbsp. sweet cream

Just as cake is done, add ½ cup coconut to above mixture and spread on cake. Broil about 5 minutes. Watch carefully, baking just until it is brown.

Waldorf Astoria Red Cake

This cake is so dense you won't miss the chocolate! I recommend making the cake several days ahead as it improves in the refrigerator and is best on the second or third day.

For the cake:

1 cup shortening – ½ oleo & ½ Crisco
1-1/2 cups sugar
2 eggs
1 oz. red food color (2 tbsp.)
2 tbsp. water
1 cup buttermilk
1 tbsp. vinegar
2 tbsp. cocoa
dash of salt
1 tsp. vanilla
2 ½ cups flour, sift together with 1 tbsp. cornstarch
1 tsp. soda

🍃 Cream shortening and sugar, then add eggs. Mix food coloring with water and cocoa and add to the above, then add flour alternating with buttermilk and salt. Add vanilla, and add vinegar and soda very last.

🍃 Pour into (2) 8" round cake pans that have been greased. Bake until toothpick inserted comes out clean, about 25 – 30 minutes.

Frosting:

      2 sticks butter – NOT oleo
      2 cups milk
      6 tbsp. flour
      1 cup Crisco
      2 cups confectioner's sugar or a little more
      2 tsp. vanilla

Put milk and flour in a pan, cook until thick and paste-like. Cool in refrigerator. In another bowl, whip butter, Crisco, sugar, and vanilla. Whip both mixtures together until creamy. Cool 20 minutes in refrigerator, then frost cake.

I usually double the frosting recipe and cut the cake layers in half horizontally with dental floss and frost four layers.

Fountain at Ann Bancroft Library at New College

Walking on Stars

Sailors black moon, Clouds of stars,
    Slice the mirrored sea
I walk on a star
    And change my life to be
My eyes are wide open
    For tis not a dream
For walking on stars
    Is easy for me
The sea is the door
    The stars, each a key
Choose the right star
    Adventure for thee
That night will come
    When your star meets the sea
Hesitate!! Adventure lost
    Life's boredom for thee
I wait and I wonder
    When that one night will be
When I walk my last star
    Into eternity

by Sam Lesko

Index

Photo Linda Thomas

Alexandra Palm

219

221

Index by Restaurant

Order Form

Please send _____ copy (ies) of

Chef du Jour

Name: _____

Address: _____

City: _____

State: _____ Zip: _____

Quantity: _____ at 19.00 = _____

$2.50 x _____ = _____

Total Amount Enclosed: _____

Send check or money order to:

Strawberry Press
3712 Woodmont Drive
Sarasota, Florida 34232
Email: Chefpress@aol.com